The 2012 Elections in Florida

Obama Wins and Democrats Make Strides in Downticket Races

Robert E. Crew, Jr. and
Mary Ruggiero Anderson

PATTERNS AND TRENDS IN FLORIDA ELECTIONS

University Press of America,® Inc.
Lanham • Boulder • New York • Toronto • Plymouth, UK

Contents

List of Figures

List of Tables

I

The 2012 Presidential Election
in Florida

Chapter One

An Overview

THE FLORIDA PRESIDENTIAL CONTEST IN 2012

In some part all elections are judgments on prior administrations and office-holders. When it voted for Barack Obama in 2008, the Florida electorate rendered a negative judgment on George W. Bush and the Republican Party, particularly their handling of the nation's economy (Abramson, Aldrichm, and Rhode 2012; Crew and Bayliss, 2011). Two years later, in 2010, voters in the state had second thoughts and retracted some of their faith in President Obama and the Democratic Party. In that election, Floridians chose Republicans for all five statewide electoral positions; US Senate, Governor, Attorney General, Chief Financial Officer and Commissioner of Agriculture. In addition, Republicans picked up four seats in the state's congressional delegation and enough positions in state legislative races to give them super majorities in both houses of the state legislature (Crew, 2012). Again the reason was the Democrats' perceived handling of the economy.

The 2012 election reaffirmed Florida's faith in its 2008 decision when for the first time since 1944 Floridians re-elected an incumbent Democratic president. Simultaneously they retracted to some extent their decision in 2010 to turn over the state's political apparatus almost completely to the Republicans. In the races for US Congress, the Democrats picked up 3 seats and in the Florida Legislature they were successful in adding to their totals in both the House of Representatives and in the State Senate. They also re-elected the only Democrat serving in a state-wide office, US Senator Bill Nelson. This book describes the nature of this election. It begins with a discussion of the 2012 presidential primary and the subsequent presidential election in Florida, proceeds to a discussion of the US Senate race, the races for US Congress and the races for the Florida State Legislature. Since no-one challenged the incumbent Democratic president, the only presidential primary was on the Republican side.

Chapter Two

The Nomination Process

REPUBLICAN PRESIDENTIAL PRIMARY

As is usual in cases where a party has no incumbent running for re-election, the presidential election season opened in 2011 with a relatively large number of Republican candidates declaring their candidacy to be their party's nominee. These were Mitt Romney, the former Governor of Massachusetts, Rick Perry, the sitting Governor of Texas, Rick Santorum, former U.S. Senator from Pennsylvania, Newt Gingrich, former Speaker of the U.S. House of Representatives, Ron Paul, U.S. Congressman from Texas, Michelle Bachman, U.S. Representative from Minnesota, Jon Huntsman, former Governor of Utah and Ambassador to China in the Clinton Administration, Tim Pawlenty, former Governor of Minnesota, Herman Cain, former CEO of Godfather's Pizza, Buddy Roemer, former Governor of Louisiana, Haley Barbour, former Governor of Mississippi and Thaddeus McCotter, an incumbent U.S. Congressman from Michigan.

Not all the candidates named above made it to the Florida primary. Prior to the first events in the primary season– the Iowa Straw Poll, the Iowa caucus, the New Hampshire primary, the Florida Straw Poll and the South Carolina primary- both Buddy Roemer and Haley Barbour abandoned their quests. As subsequent events came and went, other candidates emerged as front runners and then fell back. Initially considered a strong contender, former Minnesota Governor Tim Pawlenty dropped out after an unimpressive showing in the Iowa Straw Poll in August, 2011. Herman Cain, who led the race briefly after a surprise victory in the Florida Straw Poll in September, 2011 withdrew in December after allegations regarding sexual improprieties. The winner of the Iowa Poll, Michele Bachman, was unable to capitalize on her victory in the subsequent Iowa caucus and dropped out of the race after drawing support from only 5% of those voters. Thaddeus McCotter, never a serious candidate, joined her. Shortly after his declaration of candidacy in August of 2011, Governor Rick Perry of Texas shot to the top of the polls but dropped out in January 2012 after a series of gaffes in the television debates led to poor showings both in the Iowa caucus and in the subsequent New Hampshire primary. Jon Huntsman also withdrew after the New Hampshire race.

Models predicting the winners of presidential primaries (Randall, Dowdle ,and Steger. 2001; Norrander, 2000) estimated that Mitt Romney would emerge from this group as the Republican standard bearer and while the prediction ultimately proved accurate, the road to victory was a "long strange trip," that was influenced substantially by the candidates' activities and their performances in Florida.

In evaluating his potential, political analysts saw as advantages Mitt Romney's experience in the 2008 presidential contest, his organizational structure, his fund raising capabilities, and his standing in public opinion polls. They also noted, however, his lack of support from a crucial segment of the Republican Party coalition, evangelical and social conservatives. As the primary played out, these conservatives fought to find an alternative to Romney and the race became one between him and a series of "anti-Romneys" referred to as the "flavor of the month." At various points in the campaign Romney ran behind in the polls, shared the lead with or lost electoral contests to Herman Cain, Rick Perry, Newt Gingrich, Michelle Bachman and Rick Santorum. In the Spring of 2011 before the campaign truly began, Romney also "tied or trailed Sarah Palin, Mike Huckabee and Donald Trump" (Jones, 2012)

Throughout these events, four candidates continued their campaigns: Romney, Newt Gingrich, Rick Santorum and Ron Paul. In polls of likely Republican voters taken between December, 2011 and April, 2012, Romney was always among the leaders but fell behind or shared the lead with both Gingrich and Santorum at various points. Ron Paul never led in these polls but maintained steady support at about 12% throughout the time period.

In the first delegate selection event, the Iowa caucus, Romney appeared to have justified his claim as the strongest candidate to be the Republican nominee when the initial returns from the state gave him a razor-thin eight-vote margin over Rick Santorum. The victory reinforced his frontrunner status and gave him substantial momentum going into the New Hampshire primary, which he also won, apparently making him the first non-incumbent Republican in modern history to win the first two contests of the election cycle. As the campaign headed to South Carolina, Romney was also in the lead in that state and seemed poised to wrap up the nomination before the Florida primary. Two things occurred to alter these expectations.

First, revised figures from the Iowa caucus showed that Rick Santorum, and not Mitt Romney, had won that contest, by thirty four votes. Second, Newt Gingrich "came out of nowhere" in the last two days of the South Carolina primary to win that race by 40.4% to 27.8% for Romney. Rick Santorum got 17% of the vote and Ron Paul 13%. In the aftermath of these two events, the Florida primary took on increased importance.

THE LEAD-IN TO THE FLORIDA PRIMARY

The 2008 Republican primary in Florida was seen in its immediate aftermath as the defining moment of that race and "by this point John McCain had effectively ended the bids of all his rivals" (Abramson, Aldrich, and Rhode, 2012). In 2012 this same primary, held January 29, was equally definitive, but was not so recognized. Nevertheless, while the losers in the race continued their quest into April, Mitt Romney's substantial victory in Florida effectively ended their chances of becoming the Republican nominee. The following describes the lead-in to and the outcome of this race.

The candidates contended for a huge prize in Florida. It is the fourth largest state in the nation, sends 99 delegates to the Republican National Convention and is highly visible in national politics and extremely important to the electoral fortunes of both political parties. This visibility was enhanced in the 2012 election year when nationally televised debates among the Republican candidates were aired in both Orlando and in Jacksonville and a non-binding straw poll of Republican party regulars was conducted, also in Orlando. Subsequently, the Republican National Convention was held in Tampa. The debates and the straw poll had important effects on the outcome of the primary election.

Aware of their prominence, and in violation of national party rules, Florida Republicans sought, in both the 2008 and the 2012 elections, to capitalize on their stature by moving the date of their primary from April to January 29, putting the state ahead of all but Iowa, New Hampshire and South Carolina. Although this move was sanctioned by the national Party – Florida lost half its delegates to the national convention and was awarded inferior seating and poor hotel options at the national convention held in their own state - Florida Republicans achieved two desired purposes: ensuring that they would have an important influence on the selection of the Party's presidential candidate, and making certain that substantial amounts of money would be expended in the state during the primary campaign.

THE FLORIDA PRESIDENTIAL PRIMARY:
ROMNEY VS. GINGRICH

All of the Republican candidates recognized the importance of the Florida primary to their chances for victory and all paid verbal homage to competing in the state. Some candidates, however, did more to enhance their chances than did others. Mitt Romney and Newt Gingrich campaigned aggressively while neither Rick Santorum nor Ron Paul even aired broadcast television in the state, an absolute must for an effective campaign in Florida's huge land area covered by 10 separate media markets. Mitt Romney, in particular, started early, developed a large and sophisticated campaign organization in the state and expended substantial monetary resources.

Mitt Romney Campaign

The Romney organization opened its doors on June 1, 2011 in its Tampa headquarters and began building on efforts begun in his 2008 campaign. The campaign had five full-time staffers in the state and three offices in addition to the Tampa headquarters. It had county chairs in place in all 67 counties in Florida and volunteers who worked off voter lists collected four years earlier when Romney came in second to John McCain. (Friedman, 2012). The campaign also developed a micro-targeting schema that gave a numerical score of the likelihood of voting for Romney to each Republican in Florida.

The State of Florida allows voters to cast ballots before Election Day in two ways, by "no fault" absentee ballot and in "early voting" scheduled the last 10 days before Election Day. Large numbers of Floridians have taken advantage of this process since its creation in 2002 and political campaigns have made these voters the target of sophisticated voter contact efforts. They were the initial focus of the Romney campaign. Using micro-targeting scores developed early in the campaign, Romney's staff was able to identify and "chase" the absentee ballot requests of likely supporters or those his system had classified as persuadable. (Morrissey, 2012). More than half-a-million Republicans requested absentee ballots in 2012 and each received a brochure in the mail urging support for Romney, one or two phone calls with the same message and perhaps a knock on the door by a Romney campaign staffer, if still holding on to the ballot close to Election Day (Falcone, 2012).

This "ground" effort provided a foundation for an aggressive television strategy that was funded by millions from both the Romney organization and Restore Our Future, the Super PAC led by Romney's former political director, Carol Forti. The first Romney ads went on the air on January 3, the date of the Iowa caucus and featured three English language ads and one in Spanish. The ads in English included a short biographical sketch, one that highlighted the moral responsibility of addressing the national debt and another extolling Romney's business experience. The Spanish ad touted his support in the Cuban-American community. (Hayes, 2012). Despite apparent positivity, nearly all of the pro-Romney ads were focused not on himself but on his opponents, and invariably Romney's positive messages were tied to attacks on Newt Gingrich. For example, Florida was one of the states hit hardest by the housing crisis and Romney used statements about this crisis to slam Gingrich for his past ties to Freddie Mac, the giant housing finance organization. The ad said Gingrich "cashed in" with Freddie Mac, while Florida families lost everything in the housing crisis." His overall strategy mimicked the one that had been successful against Gingrich in Iowa; blitz him with negativity.

Newt Gingrich Campaign

In contrast to the organization created by political consultants hired by Mitt Romney, the Gingrich campaign in Florida grew out of his business, Newt, Inc. In 2005, Gingrich had opened Gingrich Communications in Miami which promoted his appearances and films and in 2009 started a Spanish-language web site called the Americano. When he became a presidential candidate in 2011, Newt's two-person staff in Miami became the Gingrich campaign in Florida. It was not until mid-December of that year that Gingrich began to hire political staff in Florida (Morrissey, 2012) and not until January 13 that he opened his first campaign office in Orlando. And it was not until Gingrich's success in the South Carolina Primary that his organization truly became viable.

"In interviews, Gingrich volunteers described a late explosion of activity after the South Carolina debate," (Sarlin, 2012). Gingrich for President offices were open in 7 locations, employed 14 paid staff and claimed to have at least 5,000 volunteers. Nevertheless, his late start put Gingrich very much behind Romney in the contest for early and absentee ballots. He had no micro-targeting program, relying instead on automated survey calls to identify Republican voters and to pinpoint their first and second choices in the race. Those who were identified as undecided were put in a queue to receive a live call from a volunteer and callers were invited to improvise the message used to persuade them for Gingrich. (Morrissey, 2012) In addition, a volunteer from Texas who mobilized a group of 30 others came to Florida with a canvassing tool that turned out to be incompatible with the campaign's data base. (Issenberg, 2012). The group identified the preferences of 48,000 voters but these data were never merged into the campaign's database and therefore were never contacted. The group leader said, "It wasn't because we didn't have enough time. It's because we weren't working with a campaign."

The former Speaker of the House came into Florida on the wave of his victory in South Carolina and "wanted to position himself as a front runner who floats above the fray" (Altman 2012). Subsequently, he identified the elements of what he thought would be a winning coalition: "Hispanics, Zionist Jews, disgruntled former employees of the hollowed-out aeronautics industry, Tea Party members and conservatives in the state's south and panhandle." (Ibid) He hoped to motivate these groups "by tailoring his speeches to fit the fears and fantasies of each," and by demonstrating that he, and not Mitt Romney, best represented the conservative instincts of the Republican Party. He anticipated doing well in two televised debates that were to be held in Jacksonville and in Tampa, a forum that he had exploited to great effect in South Carolina, and as he left South Carolina he secured a $5 million donation to his Super PAC from a billionaire supporter that provided the base for a modest television campaign.

THE FLORIDA PRESIDENTIAL PRIMARY: RICK SANTORUM AND RON PAUL

Neither Ron Paul not Rick Santorum made much of an organized effort to compete in the Florida primary. Ron Paul did not even campaign in the state in the traditional manner. He did not create a campaign organization nor announce any campaign leadership or supporters. He didn't hold a single event in the state and did not spend a single dollar on advertising. He *did* participate in the two televised debates held in Tampa and in Jacksonville, but even there made little effort to aggrandize himself to particular segments of the Republican Party coalition. He used the debates instead to articulate his libertarian message of "a sound monetary system, a gold standard, as it is under the Constitution, and a foreign policy based on strength which rejects the notion that we should be the policeman of the world and that we should be a nation builder" (Hohmann, 2012).

Like Ron Paul, Rick Santorum also made little effort in Florida and suffered from poor fundraising and weak ground operations. He did not announce a campaign team until two weeks before the primary date and actually left the state the weekend before the primary to go home and prepare his income tax records to be released to the public. Drawing on evangelical religious organizations, he did develop a grass roots field organization and scheduled several campaign events; some of which were interrupted by the illness of one of his daughters. He made no effort to "chase" absentee voters, but did participate in the two televised debates, while his performance in the debates was reviewed favorably (Jackovics, 2012).

THE OUTCOME OF THE REPUBLICAN PRESIDENTIAL PRIMARY

When the results from the Florida primary were compiled on January 29, Mitt Romney had defeated Newt Gingrich by over 14 percentage points and the remaining candidates by larger percentages. The final totals were 46.4% for Romney, 31.9% for Gingrich, 12.3% for Santorum, 7% for Ron Paul and 1.3% for other candidates. While Gingrich won more counties than did Romney (34–33), his victories came almost exclusively in the smaller, rural counties in the north and the western panhandle of Florida while Romney dominated the larger counties in the state's population centers in South and Central Florida.

In spite of the national attention focused on the primary, Florida Republicans appeared less interested in the race than they had been in 2008 and overall turnout was down by 15% compared to that year. In 2008, about 1.95 million votes were cast in the primary. In 2012, the total was about 1.67 million or 41.2% of the eligible Republican voters.

Exit polls taken in the aftermath of the vote showed that Romney won nearly every income, age, religious, ideological, and ethnic group in the state, losing only among those who call themselves "very conservative" and those who were white evangelical Christians. His support was particularly strong among Latino voters, self-described moderates, married women and wealthier voters.

Romney achieved these results by replicating the message strategy he had employed against Gingrich in Iowa: he launched a "carpet bombing" of negative campaign ads against him that brought down Gingrich's public support. He followed this up with two strong debate performances and substantially outperformed the Gingrich campaign "on the ground."

Intent on reversing the momentum Gingrich had developed with his win in South Carolina, Romney and his Super PAC Restore our Future opened the Florida campaign by unleashing their financial firepower, spending an estimated $17 million on more than 12,000 TV ads in Florida. This compared with about $3 million and 200 ads for Gingrich and his allied Super PAC. Romney's total spending in Florida was almost half the amount that he spent throughout his entire 2008 campaign

Together the two Romney organizations bought 12,768 ads on broadcast television between the first of January, 2012 and Election Day in Florida. Ninety-nine percent (99%) of these were attacks on Newt Gingrich. (Horsey, 2012.) In fact, 68% of *all* ads run in Florida during the campaign were Romney attack ads on Newt Gingrich. In the end, Romney spent more money on negative television ads in Florida than John McCain spent on his entire 2008 primary in the state (Ibid).

Romney also outperformed Mr. Gingrich in the two debates held in Florida. Gingrich's victory in South Carolina had been attributed, primarily, to his strong debate performance in that state and to the belief among voters that his skill in this aspect of the campaign would enable him to outperform and brutally shut down President Obama in the general election. He displayed very little of this skill in the Florida debates. Many observers of the debates suggest that the Gingrich debate style is best when he is attacking his opponents and as the front runner in Florida, he was put on the defensive by effective attacks from Governor Romney and, by nearly all accounts, lost both debates.

Organizationally, Romney simply overpowered Gingrich. He had concentrated on getting his supporters to vote early and by absentee ballot and on "banking" a large percentage of the votes he needed to win prior to Election Day. His efforts succeeded. More than 600,000 people cast their ballots before the polls opened and most observers in Florida suggested that Romney won a major share of them. "The pain of the situation for Gingrich was that it turned out he was the one who really needed the early votes—he came into Florida strong and left weak—but instead lost badly among the early crowd." (The Washington Examiner, 2012).

SUMMARY

When Mitt Romney and Newt Gingrich left for the Florida primary after their battle in South Carolina, there was some uncertainty about who would be the eventual Republican nominee. In the wake of the Florida contest, this uncertainty had been resolved. Although political analysts continued to speculate on the chances of other candidates, and while he subsequently lost races to both Gingrich and to Santorum, Romney never trailed either of these candidates in the delegate count or in the public opinion polls throughout the campaign. In effect, the Florida primary laid to rest any chances that any of the other candidates had of becoming the Republican presidential nominee.

Chapter Three

The Presidential General Election Process

THE STRATEGIC CONTEXT

In 2008, the Democratic presidential candidate won Florida's electoral votes for only the third time since Lyndon Johnson carried the state against Barry Goldwater in 1964. In that race voter turnout was over 65% of the eligible population and President Obama forged a winning voting coalition consisting of young people (ages 18 to 29), African Americans, Hispanics and aging baby boomers (ages 45–64). This later group was particularly important, increasing its percentage of the total vote by 10.1% and giving the president a 5% edge over John McCain. As the 2012 election season opened and the nation's economic recovery lagged, the fundamental question for both parties was whether President Obama could maintain this 2008 coalition and its enthusiastic level of support in a state where Democrats outnumbered Republicans by about 535,000 voters, but where the Republicans dominated elective office.

The condition of the economy was the overarching issue in the campaign and the question for both candidates was how to define the economic debate. According to David Axelrod, President Obama's media advisor, the Republicans tried to define it narrowly and make the race a referendum on Obama's economic management. This was particularly the case in Florida where unemployment figures were higher than in the nation as a whole. The Democrats, on the other hand, wanted to define the economic debate more broadly and make the race a choice between two visions of how to provide economic security for the middle class (Jamieson, 2013). In so doing, they hoped to motivate their voters and duplicate their '08 turnout figures.

Both the Democrats and the Republicans expected the race to be close and neither expected substantial breakthroughs over the course of the campaign. Advisors to both candidates also said they were comfortable with where they stood as the campaign opened. David Axelrod, the President's media advisor said, "I think people are realistic about where we are. They know we're in a long, hard march" (Balz, 2012). And Stuart Sevens, Romney's chief strategist added, we're very comfortable with the reality of what this race is about, and we're not in the momentum business" (Ibid).

The expected closeness of the race made turnout of the respective parties' bases extremely important. While both the Democrats and the Republicans focused on motivating their traditional constituencies, both parties were also aware of the fragility of the voting habits of important groups within the Democratic coalition (women, young people, minority populations, those who are less well-off) and both targeted them in their campaigns, in somewhat different ways. The Obama strategy hinged on a massive ground campaign that will be described later in this book.

The Republicans also mounted a substantial outreach effort targeted to their base, but also took steps that diminished the voting prospects of President Obama's supporters. Between 2008 and 2012, the Republicans used their control of the state legislature to tighten rules regarding voter registration and voting in ways that made it difficult for many of these voters, who have inflexible work schedules, to fully exercise the power of access to the polls. They made it more difficult for ex-felons to re-gain their voting rights, they shortened the number of days for early voting, they enacted more stringent rules for the collection of signatures requesting absentee ballots, and they enacted rigorous rules requiring voter identification at the polling place. Particularly controversial was the law outlawing early voting on the Sunday before Election Day while allowing it on the previous Sunday. The change blunted a voter mobilization practice that benefits Democrats, known as "souls to the polls," that buses large numbers of people to voting sites after church services two days before the election. African Americans and to a lesser extent Latinos were more likely to use this mechanism than other groups and critics complained that many of these new laws, particularly those shortening the number of early voting days, "would lead to substantially increased lines, overcrowding and confusion at the polls, which would in turn discourage some reasonable minority voters form waiting in line to cast their ballots." After the election, evidence compiled by academic and legal researchers in Florida confirmed these fears (Herron and Smith, 2014).

As had been the case in the election of 2008, Florida was essential to the electoral chances of the Republicans. Given the configuration of partisanship existent in the nation in 2012, the Republicans could not put together enough electoral votes to win the election unless it won Florida. Democrats on the other hand had a variety of "paths to victory." This fact created a different kind of imperative for the two parties, but both campaigned as if the State was critical to their election.

POSITIONING, TARGETING, AND MESSAGE

Candidates for political office design their messages around the context in which they find themselves or the "hand they are dealt." (Sides and Vavreck, 108). Although both campaigns in a particular race face identical circumstances, the meaning of these circumstances is different for the two candidates. For example, in 2012 the condition of the economy—not very good—was precisely the same for both candidates, but the meaning of this fact was different for Barack Obama than it was for Mitt Romney. The Obama campaign was forced to defend its efforts to remedy the problems involved and to try to shift the focus of the election to a different issue. The Romney campaign wanted to emphasize the problems in the economy and to blame the president for the bad times. Thus, the presidential campaigns of Barack Obama and Mitt Romney adopted contrasting positions and projected different messages.

The Obama campaign positioned the President as having made progress in spite of a very tough environment and argued that voters should stick with him because his economic plan was working. He articulated this message in the slogan, "Forward," and offered a "retooled message on health care tied to Medicare, a clearer defense of his economic record, and a concerted effort to reach Latinos and women." (Wallace, 2012). In deference to the number of seniors in Florida, Obama also emphasized his opponent's support for the Romney-Ryan Medicare plan that would have turned the program into a partially privatized system. He also tried to exploit Romney's money; how he made it and how much tax he paid on it. Finally, he latched onto Romney's shifting positions on abortion, gay rights, and health care to portray him as a flip-flopper and desperate for power.

Emphasizing his broad appeal, the president's campaign website featured 18 different groups for Obama, including women, Latinos, environmentalists and rural Americans. His administration had worked hard to include representatives from Spanish language media organization in Washington media activities and had created an entire website—*cuidadodesalud.gov*—to answer practical questions about the Affordable Care Act.

Mitt Romney focused directly on the condition of the economy and positioned himself as an experienced businessman who knew how to get it moving again. He contrasted himself against an image of President Obama as a weak leader who had failed to assert American interests and values abroad and who did not understand how the economy worked and therefore had failed to revitalize it. He criticized the President for failing to reduce unemployment and the deficit after running a campaign in 2008 that was fiercely critical of government spending under President Bush. He described "Obama's Florida" as a state with "8.6% unemployment, record foreclosures, 600,000 more Floridians in poverty" (Klas and Olorunnipa, 2012). He adopted the slogan; "Believe in America," in order to suggest that the US was a great country that simply needed new leadership. His website featured 9 different groups, with appeals to lawyers, Catholics and Polish Americans (Wallace, 2012).

HOW THE DEMOCRATS CAMPAIGNED

The Obama Ground Game

In the aftermath of the 2008 presidential campaign in Florida, former Florida Republican state chairman Tom Slade said "Bar none, he (Obama) has the best political organization for a presidential campaign I have ever seen here." (Lizza, 2008) He opened about 100 field offices in the state, had about 350 paid staff and recruited close to 250,000 volunteers (Stratton, 2008). By the end of that campaign someone from the Obama organization had either called or talked to in person more than 15% of those who voted in the 2008 election in Florida (MSMBC. 2008).

Many people attributed the president's 2008 victory in the state to this organization and the Democrats were determined to build on this performance in 2012.Thus, rather than closing their doors upon the completion of the campaign as is the common practice, the Obama organization anticipated a 2012 re-election campaign, maintained its on-the- ground presence in Florida and around the nation between 2008 and 2012 and worked hard to upgrade its technological capacity. "Chicago had 4 years to build a superior army and strategy, knowing the rivals would have to go through a long primary and would have very little time to build anything to match it." (Tomi and Ahonen. 2012. While the team was fully digital and using social media in 2008, it spent four years to build and revise and expand their system.

The Obama ground game included a technological component named Narwhal and a field staff. At the insistence of the campaign's Chief Technology Officer, Harper Reed, the technology team was housed internally, rather than dividing the enterprise among outside consultants.

Narwhal included "Gordon," a telephone-based tracking and get-out-the-vote system, and "something to give the campaign voter insights all throughout the campaign season" (Ahonen, 2012). It included an in-house polling operation that reportedly included a respondent panel of 29,000 voters in Florida and each of the battleground states. This is by two orders of magnitude more accurate than anything any professional pollster ever runs. "It was also a massive election simulation tool that could simulate anything related to the campaign, what if one of the candidates had a heart attack, what if there was a blizzard on voting day, what if there was a military scandal and the military vote support suddenly lost, etc. The Obama team ran—get this— 2 MILLION simulations through Narwhal. They knew every conceivable scenario, well before it played" (Ahonen, 2012). Finally, it was a system which linked disparate computer programs together and an Election Day app directed toward younger voters who often do not have landlines or cannot be reached by cellphone. By mid-August, 2012, this app had been downloaded by 1 million people (Kranish, 2012).

The mechanism for the continuity between 2008 and 2012 on the ground was a community organizing project called Organizing for America. Supported by the Democratic National Committee and directed in Florida by Ashley Walker who had been the state director for Obama for America in 2008, the organization sought initially to mobilize supporters for President Obama's legislative priorities as he began his presidency. Eventually the organization played a role in the midterm elections of 2010—it provided ground support for Democratic gubernatorial candidate Alex Sink—and subsequently became the ground campaign for the Obama for America re-election effort in 2012.

While the 2008 Obama for America ground game had been an exceptional effort, Jeremy Bird, Obama's national field director said that the 2012 organization makes '08 look like "amateur ball." Ultimately, in Florida, "Obama's campaign had far more people on the ground, for longer periods and backed by better data. They had more staff in Florida than we had in the country, and for longer," said Romney advisor Ron Kaufman (Kranish, 2012). The Obama ground organization opened 106 field offices in Florida, (Ball, 2012) hired nearly 800 full-time staff and had a $50 million dollar budget (Waler, 2012). A targeted ground game directed at the 50,000 Latinos who turn 18 in each month was also created (Ross,2012). Much of the money for the ground organization came from large sums transferred from the DNC and the Obama campaign to Florida's State Democratic Party (Blumenthal, 2012).

A major feature of the Obama field offices, and one that was viewed as an advantage by political scientists who studied the campaign, was that they were managed by the Obama campaign and devoted almost entirely to the president's re-election. This strategy was in contrast to the Republican offices which were managed by the Republican National Committee and were devoted almost entirely to local Republican candidates with little presence for Romney (Sides Vaverck, 2013). Other organizations, the AFL-CIO, Naral Pro-Choice America, the Sierra Club and the League of Conservation Voters, also sent people door-to-door in an effort to help the President (Mullins, 2012).

One product of the Obama ground campaign was "deep" voter contact. Each Obama worker was to be responsible for about 50 voters in key precincts over the course of the campaign. While both campaigns had similar levels of overall contact, the in-person contact of the Obama campaign beat that of the Romney campaign by 3–2 (Kranish, 2012). And the presidential campaign augmented these activities in Florida with multiple trips to the state. *FairVote* put the number at 17 trips by President Obama (8) and Vice President Biden (9). (FairVote, 2012) and Dan Lipka (2012) of the *Washington Post* showed 26 for the President and 38 for Mitt Romney. The first of these trips was announced at the Democratic National Convention and was a two-day, four-city bus tour throughout the state.

The effect of the President's ground game in Florida was profound. In a path breaking analysis of these activities by political scientists John Sides and Lynn Vaverck (2013), the authors found that "placing one field office in a county was worth about as much as an advertising advantage of roughly 3 additional ads per person on the day before the election" (220). And that "overall, we estimate that Obama gained roughly an additional 248,000 votes from his field operation. Given where those votes were located, we estimate that Florida would have been lost by a very narrow margin" in their absence.

The Obama Air War

As had been the case in Florida in the 2008 election campaign, the television advertising campaign for both the Obama and the Romney campaigns in 2012 was massive. It was also historic in terms of number of ads run and dollars spent by both sides. The Obama campaign produced more than 106 unique TV spots during the campaign, 72.5% of which mentioned Mitt Romney by name (Dwyer, 2012). Florida, as the biggest and most expensive battleground state got the most attention from the campaigns. Data collected by Kantar Media/CMAG show that the Obama campaign and its allies expended $78 million dollars in Florida on national broadcast and cable ads, 85% of which were classified as negative (Andres, 2012; Kealing and Yourish. 2012; Bohn 2012). The Wesleyan University Media Project which tracks spending on political ads concluded that the Obama campaign consistently aired more ads than the Romney campaign, while spending less for these ads.

The state of the American economy dominated the attention of both presidential television campaigns, with Obama focusing on how much the economy had improved while he was president and Mitt Romney portraying how poor the health of the economy was under the President. Nevertheless, both candidates also devoted attention to other topics. For the Obama media campaign the targets were Hispanic voters, women, African Americans and middle class voters.

By early June, the campaign had spent nearly $2 million in Hispanic ads airing in Florida, Nevada and Colorado (Naylor, 2012). Reflecting great sympathy to differences in style and culture among Hispanic voters, Obama's Spanish-language spots were highly positive and warm-feeling. In addition, they were distinctive in response to specific Latino audience. In Florida, home to large Cuban and South American immigrant populations as well as Americans from Puerto Rico, the ads feature Cuban, Puerto Rican and South American supporters, as opposed to the Mexican-American supporters who were featured in ads in Western states.

The Obama campaign also attacked Mitt Romney's positions on a number of issues important to women and to voters who support abortion rights. One ad, titled "The Same" accused Mr. Romney of promising to get rid of Planned Parenthood and of backing proposals that would take away a woman's right to choose. It lauded Mr. Obama's efforts to defend Planned Parenthood. Other ads, "Decision'" and "What He'll Do," also depicted Romney saying he would not fund Planned Parenthood and that he thought Roe v. Wade should be overturned. Both of the later ads ran in Tampa and West Palm Beach and were components of the President's final ad buy in the 2012 campaign (Dyer, 2013).

Throughout the campaign, Obama also tried to keep in front of the American public Mitt Romney's supposed indifference to and lack of contact with America's middle class. Two ads focused on this topic, "No One Was Looking" and "Firms." The first of these two ads was lifted entirely from a video secretly recorded at a Romney fundraiser that showed Mr. Romney saying "there are 47% of the people who will vote for the president no matter what…who are dependent upon government . . . who believe that government has a responsibility to care for them. And so my job is not to worry about those people. I'll never convince them they should take personal responsibility."

The second ad, "Firms" was widely cited as the most effective spot of the electoral cycle. (Siddiqul, 2012). It depicted Mr. Romney singing "America the Beautiful," while showing news reports that claimed his firm, Bain Capital, shipped American jobs to China and Mexico, that Romney had personal wealth and investments in Switzerland, Bermuda and the Cayman Islands and that as Governor of Massachusetts, he sent state jobs to India.

HOW THE REPUBLICANS CAMPAIGNED

The Romney Ground Game

In something akin to the Democrats who spent four years improving the 2008 version of their ground operation, the Romney organization, designed to identify voters and get them to the polls, was also built on a previous campaign organization, the RNC Victory grassroots organization that comes together each electoral cycle to assist Republican candidates and in presidential election years is buttressed by the campaign organization of the party's presidential candidate. Given the circumstances left by the McCain campaign in 2008, the Romney organization was forced to build almost from scratch; and it did a good job. Outside observers said "Romney's ground game was a whole generation ahead of McCain's in 2008" (Ahonen).

The Romney ground organization, like that of the Obama organization, was composed of a field staff and a computerized system designed to help identify potential Republican voters and get them to the polls on Election Day. The Romney computer system was named ORCA since Romney wanted to beat Obama and his Narwhal machine and "the only known predator in nature (other than man) that hunts the Narwhal is the killer whale Orca." (Ahonen, 2012).

The ORCA system was intended to enable volunteers in polling places around Florida and the nation to report which voters had turned out so that Republican voters who had not yet voted could be targeted for last minute efforts to get them to the polls. It was designed to work on a variety of devices, including iPhones and iPads, Android phones and tablets and Black-Berry phones. It consisted of 11 back-end database servers and a single web server and application server providing the front end. The servers were all housed in Boston. According to the campaign, ORCA would identify how between 18 and 23 million people had voted on Election Day, providing the most accurate ballot projections ever. In a training call for Republican volunteers on October 31, a staff member said "there's nothing that the Obama team, there's nothing that the Obama campaign, there's nothing that President Obama himself can do to even come close to what we are putting together here." (Sean Gallaher, 2012).

Despite this assessment, ORCA proved to be a disaster when implemented. A private sector web developer in Florida who worked as a volunteer in the Romney organization in that state described the system's multiple problems to *Business Insider* and concluded that "the end result was that 30,000+ of the most active and fired-up volunteers were wandering around confused and frustrated when they could have been driving people to the polls, phone-banking, walking door-to-door, etc. We lost by fairly small margins in Florida, Virginia, Ohio and Colorado. If this had worked could it have closed the gap? I sure hope not for my sanity" (Ekdahl, 2012).

The Romney field staff organization also differed from that of President Obama; it was smaller and managed differently. Romney opened 47 offices around the state and all were components of the Republican National Committee's coordinated effort to boast Republican candidates up and down the ticket. The RNC saw this as an advantage since the local campaigns did not duplicate efforts and the national organization was able to begin building its ground operation even before the Republican primaries chose Romney as its candidate. The RNC's political director, Rick Wiley, said that the proliferation of field operations by the Obama campaign was a symbol of a liberal big-government mentality. "They think 'if we put up 100 offices in this state, we're going to win.' We take a smaller, smarter approach, just like we do for government." (Ball, 2012) The downside of the Republican strategy was that campaign offices were devoted almost entirely to local candidates with little presence for Romney (Ibid).

The differences between the Romney and Obama field offices had substantial on-the-ground consequences. First, the numbers of individuals and offices put into place by Obama made a difference. As Rich Beeson the Romney political director said after the election, "now I know what they were doing with all the staff and offices. They were literally creating a one –to- one contact with voters" (Kranish, 2012). As a result of this kind of interaction political scientists (Sides and Vavreck, 2012) concluded that "Obama's field operation was more effective than Romney's. Our best guess is that Romney would have needed two field offices in a county to match the effect of one of Obama's offices; all else equal" (Sides and Vavreck, 220).

The Romney Air War

Reflecting the importance of Florida to Mitt Romney's presidential chances, his campaign lavished money and attention on television ads designed to influence the state's electorate. According to Kantar/CMAG, Mr. Romney and his supporters produced more than 100 individual TV ads, and spent $93 million to air them in Florida, the largest amount of money spent on behalf of either candidate in any state in 2012. Roughly 91% of these ads were negative in tone. (Wilson, Keating, and Yourish 2012)

Pursuing his strategy of turning the election into a referendum on Obama's economic performance, Romney's television ad war tried to convince Floridians that the economy was in the tank, that President Obama had not done enough to improve it and that he (Romney) had the business background that would enable him to make the decisions necessary to get the nation back on track. Four of the five ads labeled by the Brookings Institute as the best of the Romney ads focused on some element of the economy and/ or on Obama's inability to improve it. These included ads titled "The Romney Plan," "Fiscal Discipline," "Stand Up to China," and "Excuses" (West 2012).

A necessary strategy for any presidential campaign whose candidate benefits from poor economic conditions, Romney's claim that Obama had crippled the economy was appropriate messaging. Nevertheless, by June, 2012 Florida's unemployment rate had dropped for eleven months straight and the state's governor, Rick Scott, had begun issuing press releases praising the decline and asking people to "spread the news" on social media (Reeve, 2012). Put in an awkward position by these press releases, Romney first asked Scott to stop issuing them and subsequently requested him to say "the state's jobless rate could improve faster under a Romney presidency" (Ibid).

In addition to attacks on President Obama's handling of the nation's economy, the Romney campaign and its allies ran additional ads that appealed to the social conservative elements of the Republican base. One of these was a charge that President Obama had gutted the work requirements on welfare. Titled "Can't Afford Another Term," the ad said "if you want to know President Obama's second term agenda, look at his first: gutted the work requirement for welfare, doubled the number of able-bodied adults without children on food stamps." A second, a web ad produced by Karl Rove's American Crossroads Super Pac, blasted the president over his administration's botched response to the terrorist attack on the US Consulate in Libya.

Most of the money for Romney's television campaign in Florida came from outside groups such as American Crossroads, Crossroads GPS and the Koch –brothers-backed Americans for Prosperity. Seventy three percent of all ads supporting Mr. Romney came from organizations such as these (Montanaro, 2012). We reported earlier that the Obama campaign consistently aired more ads than the Romney campaign, while spending less for these ads. One reason for this is that his campaign funded most of its own advertising, which entitles it to the lowest rate charged by local television stations. By contrast, the ads supporting Romney that were paid for by his outside groups were required to pay whatever the market would bear to get their ads on the air.

SUMMARY

Success in a political campaign is determined in multiple ways: by winning the race, by improvement over previous similar campaigns and by the extent to which campaign efforts had an impact on the outcome. Evaluation against these criteria indicates that both campaigns enjoyed success.

President Obama's campaign achieved the most important outcome by winning the election, but the Mitt Romney campaign also improved upon the Republican campaign of 2008. President Obama won a very tight 50.0% to 49.1% victory and Mr. Romney improved upon the vote share of Mr. McCain by a similar .9%.

John Sides and Lynn Vavreck also demonstrate the success of President Obama's advertising strategy in Florida as well as his "ground game." The Obama strategy for buying advertising and his near parity in expenditures with Romney in the last days of the campaign, ensured that Romney was never able to achieve the necessary advertising advantage he needed in the last weeks of the campaign to overcome Obama's lead. (Sides and Vavreck, 170) In addition, Obama gained an additional 248,000 votes from his field operation and without them, "Obama would have lost Florida by a very narrow margin." (Ibid).

Chapter Four

The Presidential Election Results

Florida has cemented itself as The Battleground State in the nation. The demographic composition of Florida makes the state a microcosm of the nation as a whole, reflecting the many changing facets of the country. In fact, over the last 10 presidential elections (1976-2012), only in 1992, did Florida *not* elect the candidate who would become president.

In the election of 2012, Florida was the last state to be called and was the tightest margin of victory for Obama, winning by less than 1% (the narrowest margin of victory for all the states in 2012). Without a doubt, the presidential election results in Florida lived up to the "hype" of campaign 2012. While Obama did not need Florida to reach the necessary 270 electoral votes to claim victory, Florida none-the-less holds 29 electoral votes to be awarded to the victor and it was a long wait from Election Day, November 6, 2012 until the votes were certified on November 20, 2012,(though by November 10, most major news outlets were projecting an Obama victory, narrow though it was). By a .9 margin-- Romney carrying 49.1% to Obama's 50%--Obama won Florida's 29 electoral votes and became the first Democratic presidential candidate to win two consecutive elections in Florida since Franklin D. Roosevelt (Roper Center 2012). Obama beat Romney by 164,309 votes out of the 8,538,264 votes cast in the state. Of the 67 Florida counties, Obama won 13 compared to Romney's 54. While on the surface or looking at a county map of blue and red, there are far fewer counties that voted for Obama, it is important to bear in mind that the counties Mr. Obama carried were from high population areas such as Miami-Dade, Broward, Palm-Beach, Tampa, and Orlando.

Table 4.1.   Obama beat Romney 164,309 votes.

Candidate	Votes	Percent
Democrat Barack Obama	4,237,756	50.00%
Republican Mitt Romney	4,163,447	49.14%

Source: Florida Department of State, Division of Elections, Official Results http://doe.dos.state.fl.us/elections/resultsarchive/Index.asp?ElectionDate=11/6/2012&DATA-MODE

Table 4.2.   County by County Results for the Presidential General Election 2012

President of the United States

County	Mitt Romney (REP)	Barack Obama (DEM)
Alachua	48,797	69,699
Baker	8,975	2,311
Bay	56,876	22,051
Bradford	8,219	3,325
Brevard	159,300	122,993
Broward	244,101	508,312
Calhoun	4,366	1,664
Charlotte	47,996	35,906
Citrus	44,662	28,460
Clay	70,022	25,759
Collier	96,520	51,698
Columbia	18,429	8,462
Desoto	5,587	4,174
Dixie	5,052	1,798
Duval	211,615	196,737
Escambia	88,711	58,185
Flagler	26,969	23,207
Franklin	3,570	1,845
Gadsden	6,630	15,770
Gilchrist	5,917	1,885
Glades	2,344	1,603
Gulf	4,995	2,014
Hamilton	3,138	2,228
Hardee	4,696	2,463
Hendry	5,355	4,751
Hernando	44,938	37,830
Highlands	25,915	16,148
Hillsborough	250,186	286,467
Holmes	6,919	1,264
Indian River	43,450	27,492
Jackson	13,418	7,342
Jefferson	3,808	3,945

Lafayette	2,668	687
Lake	87,643	61,799

Source: Florida Department of State, Division of Elections, Official Results http://doe.dos.state.fl.us/elections/resultsarchive/Index.asp?ElectionDate=11/6/2012&DATA-MODE

EARLY VOTING

As noted previously, changes to early voting rules had important consequences for the election. Changes from the Republican led legislature in Florida cut the number of early votes days by nearly half in 2012 compared to 2008; from 14 days to 8 days. This has the effect of decreasing the number of early votes cast in the state from 2.6 million in 2008 to 2.4 million in 2012. Early voting tends to help Democratic candidates thus, Republicans were likely to gain from the decreased number of days allowed for early voting. Simultaneously, requests for absentee ballots increased in 2012. Republicans tend to do better than Democrats in absentee ballot results. In 2012, absentee ballots increased from 1.7 million in 2008 to over 2 million in 2012 (Caputo, M 2012). The implications to the changes are that Republicans ought to have the advantage in both early voting and absentee voting. However, that did not happen. Results below show that Democrats were able to hold on to the method that they historically captured—early voting-- and Republicans held on to absentee ballots. Democrats carried 46% of the early votes, compared to 36% by Republicans. On the other hand, Republicans carried 43% of absentee votes compared to 39% by Democrats. On the last day of early voting, a wave of voters surged to the polls, with nearly 385,000 casting ballots.

VOTER REGISTRATION AND TURNOUT

While difficult to replicate the surge in newly registered voters from 2008—which totaled over 1 million, Florida none the less saw a large increase in voter registration for 2012. 886,132 new voters registered throughout the state. The chart below depicts voter registration in Florida from 1995 to 2014.

Given the competiveness and closeness of the final results of the 2012 presidential election, it is not surprising that registration in the state in 2012 Democrats held just over 550, 000 registered voters compared to Republicans. In 2012 there were 4,263,587 registered Republicans and 4,821,859 registered Democrats. There were also 2,953,125 registered as an "other" party. These "others" should not be discounted however, as they clearly have played a role in deciding the outcome of campaigns over the last few elections, as and depicted below their numbers have steadily been increasing over time.

Table 4.3.   Early vote numbers for the Presidential General Election

Early Vote:

Party	EV Total	%
DEM	1,109,262	46%
REP	862,277	36%
IND	440,133	18%
TOTAL	2,411,672	

Absentee vote:

Party	AB Total	%
REP	885,675	43%
DEM	806,310	39%
IND	365,736	18%
TOTAL	2,057,721	

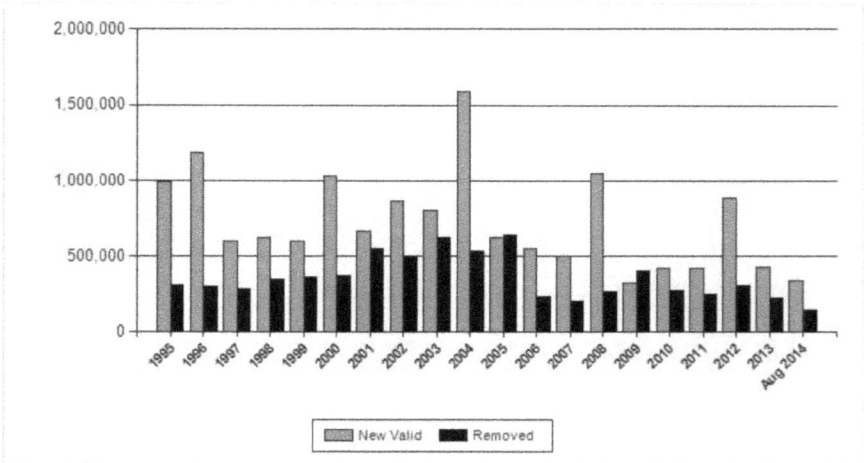

Figure 4.1.   Change in Voter Registration 1995–2014. Source: Florida Department of State, Division of Elections http://election.dos.state.fl.us/nvra/changes.asp.

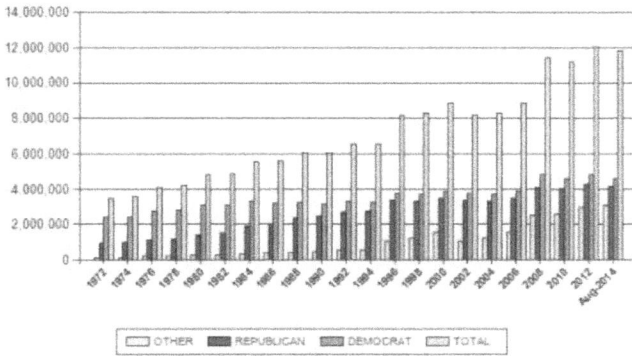

Figure 4.2. Voter Registration in Florida 1972–2014.

Turnout in the 2012 election was 71.5% this was down less than 4% from 2008 figures (75% turnout rate). There were nearly 12 million registered voters and 8.5 million cast a ballot. The county with the highest turnout was 83.3% in Collier County and the lowest was Hardee County with 59%, 26 counties had over a 75% turnout rate. The modest change in turnout as depicted below (8% or less across all counties) suggests that those turnout remained relatively stable from the 2008 to 2012 election in Florida.

Table 4.4. Voter Registration in Florida 1982-2014

Year	Republican	Democrat	Other	Total
1972	974,999	2,394,604	117,855	3,487,458
1974	1,035,510	2,438,580	147,166	3,621,256
1976	1,138,751	2,750,723	204,834	4,094,308
1978	1,178,671	2,812,217	226,299	4,217,187
1980	1,429,645	3,087,427	292,649	4,809,721
1982	1,500,031	3,066,351	299,254	4,865,636
1984	1,895,937	3,313,073	365,462	5,574,472
1986	2,038,831	3,214,753	377,604	5,631,188
1988	2,360,434	3,264,105	422,808	6,047,347
1990	2,448,488	3,149,747	432,926	6,031,161
1992	2,672,968	3,318,565	550,292	6,541,825
1994	2,747,074	3,245,518	567,006	6,559,598
1996	3,344,036	3,774,809	1,077,812	8,196,657
1998	3,327,207	3,731,367	1,268,133	8,326,707
2000	3,474,438	3,853,524	1,552,434	8,880,396
2002	3,610,992	3,956,694	1,756,873	9,324,559
2003	3,577,179	3,880,342	1,808,963	9,266,484
2004	3,954,492	4,322,376	2,199,569	10,476,437
2005	3,954,304	4,276,512	2,241,102	10,471,918
2006	3,920,201	4,196,608	2,268,797	10,385,606

2007	3,826,836	4,138,604	2,241,161	10,206,601
2008	4,106,743	4,800,890	2,504,290	11,411,923
2009	3,967,472	4,637,354	2,459,541	11,064,367
2010	4,042,393	4,611,335	2,562,010	11,215,738
2011	4,061,224	4,552,483	2,622,454	11,236,161
2012	4,263,587	4,821,859	2,953,125	12,038,571
2013	4,133,350	4,621,791	2,962,605	11,717,746
2014	4,182,775	4,627,737	3,175,916	11,986,428
2015	4,161,672	4,581,004	3,214,915	11,957,591

Table 4.5.   Voter Turnout by County 2012 vs. 2008

| County | 2012 | | | 2008 | | |
	Voter Reg	Turnout	Turnout %	Voter Reg	Turnout	Turnout %
Alachua	164,912	121,140	73.50%	154,706	126,322	81.70%
Baker	14,006	11,460	81.80%	14,172	11,156	78.70%
Bay	112,915	80,421	71.20%	110,739	81,692	73.80%
Bradford	15,491	11,719	75.70%	15,732	11,777	74.90%
Brevard	380,469	287,546	75.60%	351,488	289,931	82.50%
Broward	1,140,454	762,345	66.80%	1,008,656	739,873	73.40%
Calhoun	8,278	6,232	75.30%	8,622	6,317	73.30%
Charlotte	115,050	85,355	74.20%	118,837	86,035	72.40%
Citrus	98,639	74,543	75.60%	102,742	76,865	74.80%
Clay	132,585	97,081	73.20%	120,656	94,814	78.60%
Collier	180,560	150,346	83.30%	203,075	143,120	70.50%
Columbia	35,539	27,322	76.90%	38,272	28,360	74.10%
Desoto	16,376	9,935	60.70%	15,613	10,211	65.40%
Dixie	10,229	7,006	68.50%	10,775	7,377	68.50%
Duval	557,282	414,111	74.30%	536,588	417,666	77.80%
Escambia	198,275	149,716	75.50%	195,193	155,506	79.70%
Flagler	69,597	50,836	73.00%	60,079	49,356	82.20%
Franklin	7,174	5,537	77.20%	7,722	6,130	79.40%
Gadsden	29,625	22,638	76.40%	30,128	22,628	75.10%
Gilchrist	11,121	8,004	72.00%	10,721	7,870	73.40%
Glades	6,668	4,004	60.00%	6,584	4,293	65.20%
Gulf	9,030	7,177	79.50%	9,123	7,284	79.80%
Hamilton	7,963	5,460	68.60%	7,688	5,651	73.50%
Hardee	12,312	7,268	59.00%	11,802	7,476	63.30%
Hendry	17,264	10,324	59.80%	16,936	10,976	64.80%
Hernando	123,346	84,581	68.60%	123,013	88,624	72.00%
Highlands	62,076	42,981	69.20%	66,092	45,404	68.70%
Hillsborough	747,587	545,134	72.90%	701,464	515,983	73.60%
Holmes	11,560	8,373	72.40%	11,513	8,719	75.70%
Indian River	93,569	72,117	77.10%	90,053	71,145	79.00%
Jackson	29,003	21,094	72.70%	28,128	21,783	77.40%

Jefferson	9,517	7,838	82.40%	10,310	8,017	77.80%
Lafayette	4,568	3,443	75.40%	4,469	3,416	76.40%
Lake	201,652	151,975	75.40%	188,702	148,144	78.50%
Levy	25,053	18,550	74.00%	25,924	18,883	72.80%
Liberty	4,410	3,329	75.50%	4,304	3,337	77.50%
Madison	12,001	8,727	72.70%	12,278	8,959	73.00%
Manatee	209,468	154,263	73.60%	206,211	152,924	74.20%
Marion	223,478	162,632	72.80%	214,722	163,297	76.10%
Martin	101,835	79,453	78.00%	101,155	79,005	78.10%
Miami-Dade	1,313,850	888,033	67.60%	1,243,315	872,260	70.20%
Monroe	51,524	39,315	76.30%	50,136	40,690	81.20%
Nassau	51,607	40,755	79.00%	47,501	38,570	81.20%
Okaloosa	128,865	95,252	73.90%	129,373	96,042	74.20%
Okeechobee	19,185	12,418	64.70%	18,859	12,903	68.40%
Orange	690,645	470,192	68.10%	604,243	466,002	77.10%
Osceola	163,384	109,542	67.00%	136,544	100,925	73.90%
Palm Beach	870,186	605,268	69.60%	831,423	594,854	71.50%
Pasco	310,322	215,577	69.50%	294,431	217,115	73.70%
Pinellas	626,348	461,806	73.70%	643,423	468,700	72.80%
Polk	351,119	250,454	71.30%	332,015	246,538	74.30%
Putnam	43,581	31,571	72.40%	46,432	33,393	71.90%
Santa Rosa	116,941	77,405	66.20%	107,253	76,583	71.40%
Sarasota	277,672	208,623	75.10%	260,618	208,683	80.10%
Seminole	277,376	209,913	75.70%	259,336	206,970	79.80%
St. Johns	152,849	115,390	75.50%	131,744	106,427	80.80%
St. Lucie	175,554	123,750	70.50%	157,676	121,598	77.10%
Sumter	73,946	60,775	82.20%	59,913	49,244	82.20%
Suwannee	25,043	17,803	71.10%	24,791	17,811	71.80%
Taylor	12,585	9,231	73.30%	13,088	9,449	72.20%
Union	7,313	5,452	74.60%	7,273	5,359	73.70%
Volusia	332,556	236,215	71.00%	326,854	245,842	75.20%
Wakulla	18,501	14,748	79.70%	18,565	14,444	77.80%
Walton	38,368	28,677	74.70%	36,847	27,238	73.90%
Washington	14,668	11,120	75.80%	15,938	11,272	70.70%
Total	**11,934,446**	**8,538,264**	**71.50%**	**11,247,634**	**8,456,329**	**75.20%**

Chapter Five

Voting Behavior
in the Presidential Election

Social Groups and the Vote

Thus far, the analysis in this book has focused on voter turnout and candidate preference. Our attention will now shift to an analysis of the demographic characteristics of voters in the 2012 election. We will examine the national presidential vote as well as the vote in Florida. New York Times exit polling data demonstrate that President Obama was able to maintain support among the key groups that propelled him to his 2008 White House victory (New York Times 2012).

SEX

Obama held on to the 2008 support that he received from women voters. Overall 52% of men voted for Romney and 55% of females voted for Obama in 2012. In Florida, 52% of men voted for Romney and 53% of women voted for Obama.

RACE AND ETHNICITY

White voters supported Romney while Black voters maintained their overwhelming support of President Obama. Obama also garnered significant support among Hispanics and Asian voters. Fifty-nine percent of white voters cast their ballots in favor of Mr. Romney, however 93% of Black voters, 71% of Hispanic voters, and 73% of Asian voters provided support for President

Obama. In Florida the pattern was consistent with national trends. Mr. Romney captured 61% of the white vote, while President Obama received 95% of the Black vote and 60% of the Hispanic vote.

AGE

In 2008, then candidate Obama, energized young voters and captured their attention with his message of hope and change. The campaign's ability to turn that energy into actual votes paid off immensely with young voters overwhelmingly supporting candidate Obama over candidate McCain. A huge test in the 2012 election was whether the support would continue or wane. In 2012, young voters again supported President Obama over Mr. Romney, though support among the young did fall by about 5% points. Among those age 18-29, 60% supported Obama, of those 30-44 52% supported Obama and Mr. Romney had a slight lead among those age 45-64 with 51% supporting his candidacy and among those 65+ 56% supported Mr. Romney. In Florida, President Obama maintained his support of young voters. Among 18-29 year olds, 68% supported Obama and among 30-44 year olds 52% supported Obama. Mr. Romney held on to support of the 45-64 age group with 52% of the vote and among those 65+ he received 58% of the vote.

SUMMARY OF KEY DEMOGRAPHIC GROUPS

We will examine the breakdown of groups even further to include education, income, ideology, and more in the pages that follow, but we think it is important to pause here and draw out some conclusions regarding these key demographic groups. First, the Republican candidate Mitt Romney, picked up support from 2008 numbers in some key areas. First, in terms of sex, we saw a change of 4% for men towards Romney and 1% of women towards Romney. In terms of race and ethnicity, the Republican candidate also made gains among white voters (4%) and black voters (2%) but the Democratic candidate President Obama made gains among Hispanic (4%) and Asian voters (11%). Mr. Romney also picked up support in all age categories when compared to 2008 except among 30-44 year olds, where the support was unchanged from 2008. In Florida more specifically, Obama's support grew among women, Hispanics and those 18-44 years old while Romney's support increased among men, whites, and those 45 years of age and older. These are important changes to note because as the shifting demographics of the electorate change, candidates want and need to gain support among minorities and the younger age groups; gaining support among white voters—whose numbers in the electorate are decreasing—will not increase the likelihood of

Table 5.1. Social Characteristics of Voters and the Presidential Vote: The Nation v. Florida

	National	Florida	Percent Change from 2008 in FLORIDA
Sex	52% Romney	52% Romney	+5 Romney
Male	55% Obama	53% Obama	+1 Obama
Female			
Race and Ethnicity	59% Romney	61% Romney	+5% Romney
White	93% Obama	95% Obama	Unchanged
Black	71% Obama	60% Obama	+3% Obama
Hispanic	73% Obama		
Asian			
Age	60% Obama	66% Obama	+5% Obama
18-29	52% Obama	52% Obama	+3% Obama
30-44	51% Romney	52% Romney	+5% Romney
45-64	56% Romney	58% Romney	+5% Romney
65+			

winning presidential elections. Gains need to be garnered among minorities and young voters. If Republicans can continue to siphon off votes among black voters (as they did in 2012 by 2%) their chances in winning will increase, but they will have to increase that support and couple it with gains among other minority groups as well. While Democrats need to hold on to the gains they've made with Hispanics and Asians and regain some of the support they lost among the younger vote.

Education

Education is interesting to examine. Those with the lowest education levels and the highest education levels supported President Obama. Those with no college degree and some college and those with post graduate degrees supported Obama over Romney, while those with college degrees supported Romney. In Florida those with no college and those with post-graduate degrees supported Obama while those with some college and college degrees supported Romney. Overall though, these numbers hover right around 50%, +- 5 percent in the most extreme case.

Income

Consistent with trends in voting behavior, the Democratic candidate, President Obama had the strongest support among lower income groups compared to the Republican candidate, Mr. Romney. Obama received 63% of the vote among those making less than $30,000 and 57% of the vote among those making $30-49,999. Mr. Romney received 53% of the vote among those earning $50,000 or more and 54% of those making $100,000 or more. In Florida the pattern mirrors that at the national level.

City v. Suburbs

The President retained support among those living in cities while Mr. Romney received support in small cities and suburbs. In Florida, however, Mr. Romney received his largest support among those living in big cities and small cities, while President Obama received support among those living in mid-size cities and suburbs.

Political Party and Ideology

Studies have remained consistent over time that the single best predictor of how someone will vote is their party identification. It is no surprise then that President Obama had support among Democrats and Liberals while Mr. Romney had support among Republicans and Conservatives. However, it is among Independents and moderates where the results are more interesting . First, in terms of political party, 50% of Independents favored Mr. Romney while 45% favored President Obama. This is a gain for Republicans of 6% from 2008 nationally. In Florida, the gain was a modest 2% from 2008 among Independents with Obama capturing 50% of Independents and Romney with 47%. Second, for ideology, President Obama picked up 56% of moderates compared to 41% for Romney nationally, this is a loss of about 2% for Obama from 2008. In Florida, President Obama had 53% of moderates compared to Romney who had 46%--this was another loss for Obama of about 5% compared to 2008.

The Economy

Finally, the NYT Exit Poll asked voters about the economy. Among those who thought the economy was excellent or good, 90% voted for Obama while those who thought the economy was not so good or poor 60% voted for Romney. In Florida, where the economy was hard hit in 2008, among those who thought it was excellent or good 91% voted for President Obama and 66% voted for Romney. While these numbers taken at face value are probably not surprising, the change from 2008 is somewhat dramatic. The change among those who viewed the economy as excellent or good was a +67% shift from 2008 towards Obama and among those who viewed the economy as not so good or poor was a +21% shift towards Romney from 2008.

SUMMARY

Taken together, what is to be made of these results? First, Republicans have been making gains with some key voting groups (Blacks and young voters) nationally but these groups remain supportive of Democrats overall. In Florida, Republicans need to make gains among these key minority groups while Democrats need to continue to make gains among Hispanic voters and young voters and retain majorities of women and Black voters. Data from Florida suggest that most patterns have remained consistent with theories of voting behavior for education and income but some curious results are evident in terms of size of city. This finding may warrant further examination with additional data since it is inconsistent with national patterns. Finally, among

Table 5.2.   **Other Characteristics of Voters and the Presidential Vote: The Nation v. Florida**

	National	Florida	Percent Change from 2008 in FLORIDA
Education	51% Obama	52% Obama	+2% Romney
No college	49% Obama	50% Romney	+1% Romney
Some college	51% Romney	52% Romney	+1% Obama
College	55% Obama	53% Obama	+5% Romney
Postgrad			
Income	63% Obama	61% Obama	+2% Romney
Under 30K	57% Obama	57% Obama	+4% Romney
30-49.9K	53% Romney	55% Romney	Unchanged
50k or more	54% Romney	57% Romney	na
100K or more			
City v. Suburb	69% Obama	67% Romney	+13% Romney
Big city	58% Obama	59% Obama	+5% Obama
Mid-size city	56% Romney	61% Romney	+6% Romney
Small city	50% Romney	51% Suburbs	+3% Romney
Suburbs			
Ideology	86% Obama	86% Obama	+5% Romney
Liberal	56% Obama	53% Obama	+5% Romney
Moderate	82% Romney	78% Romney	+1% Romney
Conservative			
Political Party	92% Obama	90% Obama	+3% Obama
Democrat	93% Romney	92% Romney	+5% Romney
Republican	50% Romney	50% Obama	+2% Romney
Independent			
The Economy is	90% Obama	91% Obama	+67 Obama
Excellent/good	60% Romney	66% Romney	+21 Romney
Not so good/poor			

Independents and Moderates, Republicans have made small gains but gains none-the-less and they will need to grow that number in the future as Democrats still hold small majorities in these two groups. They will need to regain the support they lost from 2008 to hold on to these majorities. The changing demographics of the electorate warrant particular consideration as Florida is a battleground state where small shifts at the margins can have large implications nationally.

Chapter Six

Issues and Candidate Perceptions

In any election, voters' opinions about the issues affecting the country and their opinions about the candidates are relevant to electoral results. In a healthy and well-functioning democracy, issue concerns in the electorate can have meaningful implications for policy output. Indeed, the candidate that voters perceive to be better at handling particular issues may claim a mandate to follow through with his/her policy preferences (as Barack Obama did in 2009-10 when the Democratically controlled Congress passed the Affordable Health Care Act and President Obama signed it into law). Thus, it is important to understand the opinions of the public in the days leading up to an election and their opinions as they exited polling precincts. In the section that follows we will chronicle the issues that were at the forefront of voters' minds. First, we will examine data from likely voters in Florida from the Quinnipiac University Poll released October 31, 2012 just one week prior to the election. As a battleground state we are fortunate that Florida gets paid particular attention by reputable polling sources like Quinnipiac and that those results are available for us to explore in examining the 2012 Election in Florida. We will also examine exit polling data from CNN collected the day of the election.

DAYS LEADING UP TO THE ELECTION: LIKELY VOTERS IN FLORIDA

The Economy

Similar to 2008, the economy was the most important issue for likely voters. Among likely voters in Florida, 51% believed the economy was the most important problem. A distant second to the economy was health care with

15% viewing it as the most important problem followed by Medicare with 9%. Terrorism, which in 2008 followed the economy in terms of the most important problem with 10% of Florida voters choosing that issue, was last among the issues for 2012 with only 1% choosing that issue. The economy was by far the issue of greatest concern to Florida voters leading up to the election. Among Florida voters, 42% believed the national economy was getting better while 33% believed it was getting worse and 24% thought it had stayed the same. However, only 25% believed that the economy in Florida was getting worse, while 37% believed it was getting better and 36% believed it had stayed the same. Given that the economy was front and center on voters' mind who did they believe would be best at handling the economy? When asked by Quinnipiac who would do a better job on the economy 47% indicated Barack Obama while 49% indicated Mitt Romney. When we examine the various aspects of the economy such as taxes and budget deficits, voters believed Mitt Romney would do a better job with the budget deficit 53% indicating support for Romney compared to Barack Obama with 40%. In terms of taxes, voters were more evenly split; 48% believed Barack Obama would do a better job compared to 47% who believed that Mitt Romney would. Some may argue that health care and Medicare should also be considered when discussing the economy because these two programs are arguably major components of the overall US budget. Among likely voters, 52% believed Barack Obama would do a better job on health care compared to 43% for Mitt Romney and 50% believed Barack Obama would do a better job at Medicare compared to 44% for Mitt Romney. Provided these numbers, the closeness of the electoral results in Florida are really not surprising. Later we will discuss exit polling results as they relate to the economy and other issues.

Other Issues

Other issues that were of concern to voters included social issues, helping the middle class, education, terrorism, and foreign policy. When asked who they believed would do a better job handling these issues, Obama was favored for nearly all of the issues except "working with both Democrats and Republicans." This is likely due to his inability to garner bi-partisan support in his first term coupled with Mitt Romney's ability to work with a mostly Democratic legislature while he was Governor of Massachusetts. Most likely voters believed that Obama would be better for helping the middle class, foreign policy, education, terrorism, and social issues like abortion and same sex marriage. He topped Romney for all of these issues by at least 5%.

Table 6.1.   Public Opinion of Likely Florida Voters on Key Campaign Issues

Most Important Issue	Florida Likely Voters	
Terrorism	1%	
Foreign Policy	3%	
The Economy	51%	
The Budget Deficit	7%	
Taxes	4%	
Health care	15%	
Medicare	9%	
Something else	7%	
DK/NA	2%	
The economy is getter	Florida Likely Voters Nationally	Florida Likely Voters In Florida
Better	42%	37%
Worse	33%	25%
Stay the Same	24%	36%
Who would do a better job on…	Florida Likely Voters Barack Obama	Florida Likely Voters Mitt Romney
The economy	47%	49%
Taxes	48%	47%
Budget deficit	40%	53%
Health care	52%	43%
Medicare	50%	44%

Quinnipiac Poll results Oct 31, 2012. http://www.quinnipiac.edu/news-and-events/quinnipiac-university-poll/presidential-swing-states-(fl-oh-and-pa)/release-detail?ReleaseID=1812

THE DAY OF ELECTION: CNN EXIT POLLING, DATA, FLORIDA VOTERS, AND THE NATION

The results of the exit polling data conducted by CNN show a similar pattern to the data collected the previous week from Quinnipiac. This suggests that there was relatively little to no difference at all in voters opinions just prior to and the day of the election.

Table 6.2. Public Opinion of Likely Florida Voters on the Candidates

Who would do a better job on...	Florida Likely Voters	
	Barack Obama	Mitt Romney
Helping the middle class	51%	44%
Foreign policy	50%	44%
Social issues like abortion and same sex marriage	57%	34%
Education	53%	40%
Terrorism	49%	44%
Working with both Democrats and Republicans	41%	50%

Most Important Issue

The economy was overwhelmingly the issue that most concerned voters in the 2012 election. Nationally, 47% indicated the economy was their greatest concern and 62% in Florida indicated the same. The CNN exit polling data allows us to take a more nuanced look at how supporters of Obama and Romney viewed these issues. Among the 62% of Florida voters who indicated the economy was the most important issue, 46% supported Obama and 53% supported Romney. Given that the economy was the biggest concern, CNN asked "what was the biggest economic problem facing people like you?" Responses were split both nationally and in Florida between unemployment and rising prices. In Florida, 37% indicated rising prices and 36% indicated unemployment, with less than 25% combined indicating the housing market and taxes. Among those that cited unemployment as the biggest problem, Obama won their support, while those that cited taxes, supported Romney.

Candidate Quality

Despite approval ratings falling below 50% in the months leading up to the election, President Obama was able to secure a second term. In CNN exit polling data, his favorable ratings broke 50% while Mitt Romney failed to reach 50% favorable ratings. More importantly, perhaps, is that Obama's unfavorable ratings were below 50%; for a president seeking a second term this is critical. Perhaps much of Obama's ability to sustain his second term chances was that voters liked the qualities he possessed as a person. In terms of personal candidate qualities, among Florida likely voters, 54% believed Obama was honest and trustworthy compared to 47% who felt the same

Table 6.3. Exit Poll Results on Campaign Issues: National Voters vs. Florida Voters

Most Important Issue	Nation	Nation	Nation	Florida	Florida	Florida
	Total	Obama	Romney	Total	Obama	Romney
Foreign Policy	5%	56%	33%	5%	53%	45%
Deficit	15%	32%	66%	13%	30%	66%
Economy	47%	47%	51%	62%	46%	53%
Healthcare	18%	75%	24%	17%	78%	20%
Biggest Economic Problem Facing People Like You						
Housing Market	8%	63%	32%	11%	57%	43%
Unemployment	38%	54%	44%	36%	53%	47%
Taxes	14%	32%	66%	11%	40%	60%
Rising Prices	37%	49%	49%	38%	50%	48%

Source: CNN Exit Poll 2012 http://www.cnn.com/election/2012/results/state/FL/president and http://www.cnn.com/election/2012/results/race/president

about Mitt Romney. Mitt Romney, however, outdid Obama in terms of the quality of strong leadership, with 65% indicating Mitt Romney had strong leadership compared to 55% for Obama. The CNN exit polling data indicates that having "a vision for the future" was the most important of candidate qualities, 45% of those polled nationally and 32% of Floridians indicated this preference. Among those, Mitt Romney beat Obama by at least 7% points. Obama beat Romney resoundingly in the quality "cares about people" 83% to 15% in Florida and 81% to 18% nationally though that was the least important quality among Floridians.

SUMMARY

The data seem to indicate that despite a perception among voters of weak economy, approval ratings below 50%, and weaker candidate leadership qualities than his opponent, Barack Obama is genuinely "liked" and possessed qualities that went beyond your typical leadership qualities to include caring, honesty, trustworthiness, and helping others. These qualities, it seems, lifted him over the top especially compared to an opponent who was viewed strongly in terms of qualities such as leadership and a vision for the future but was somewhat "unlikeable" as a person or was perceived to be less caring, honest, and trustworthy than his opponent. Every indicator that would suggest the failure of securing a second term was present for Barack Obama

Table 6.4. Exit Poll Results on Candidate Quality: National Voters vs. Florida Voters

Most Important Candidate Quality	Nation	Nation	Nation	Florida	Florida	Florida
	Total	Obama	Romney	Total	Obama	Romney
Shares my values	27%	42%	55%	23%	40%	59%
Strong leader	18%	38%	61%	22%	40%	59%
Cares about people	21%	81%	18%	19%	83%	15%
Vision for future	45%	45%	54%	32%	46%	53%
Opinion of…						
Favorable		53%	47%		53%	49%
Unfavorable		46%	50%		45%	47%

Source: CNN Exit Poll 2012 http://www.cnn.com/election/2012/results/state/FL/president and http://www.cnn.com/election/2012/results/race/president

but he was able to win a second term in the White House. The economy trumped all other issues and voters and likely voters were of the opinion that Mitt Romney would do a better job in handling the economy by a small margin, yet he was unable to win. It seems that "other" candidate qualities and "other issues" can have a greater influence on the outcome of the election. Perhaps it is these "other issues and qualities" that are more salient to voters. These issues ignite greater passion and as a result may increase turnout. As has been chronicled in this book, voter turnout was key to an Obama victory. Research over the last 40 years has suggested, these "other issues" such health care, Medicare, social issues, and education tend to be more aligned with the concerns of the voting blocs to which Obama courted and won over—women and minorities. Coupled with his "likeability" he was able to overcome the economy and win the White House for a second term. While a first glance at the most important issue would indicate "it's the economy" taken together we see a different picture emerge. Perhaps in 2012 it was "despite the economy."

II

The Race for the U.S. Senate

Chapter Seven

The Campaign for the U.S. Senate

BACKGROUND AND CONTEXT

In 2012, Florida offered the Republicans an opportunity to gain control of the one statewide office it did not hold, the US Senate position occupied by incumbent Democrat Bill Nelson. Senator Nelson had experienced a long career in Florida politics; he served in the state legislature from 1972 to 1976, in the US Congress from 1979 to 1991 and in the position of Treasurer and Insurance Commissioner of Florida from 1994 to 2000. In 1990, he lost a race for Governor before being elected in 2000 to the US Senate seat vacated by retiring Republican Senator Connie Mack, III. He was re-elected to the position in 2006, running against Katherine Harris, the Republican state Secretary of State who gained notoriety for her role in the 2000 presidential election re-count in Florida. He is generally regarded as a moderate, with the conservative *National Journal* ranking him as such on economic issues, on matters of foreign policy and on social issues (Project Vote Smart, 2012).

From the outset of the 2012 campaign Nelson, never a dynamic campaigner, was viewed as vulnerable to Republican defeat. Two polls, one taken in December, 2011 and another in February, 2012, showed that he fell short of the 50 percent support mark against five potential Republican opponents and that he ran behind former Governor Jeb Bush (Burns, 2011). Furthermore, in 2012 he shared the ticket with President Obama, whose re-election chances were tied closely to the nature of the national and state economies.

Given his perceived vulnerability, Republicans at the national level were optimistic that Nelson could be beaten and he initially attracted a number of potential opponents. They included, at various times, Jeff Atwater, Florida's Chief Financial Officer, George LeMieux, who had served a year and a half in the Senate after being selected by Governor Charlie Crist as a temporary replacement for US Senator Mel Martinez when he resigned that seat in 2010, Connie Mack, IV a US Congressman and son of the person whose resignation in 2000 led to Nelson's ascent to his position, Mike Haridopolos, Florida State Senate President, former state Representative and House Majority Leader Adam Hasner, Mike McCalister, a retired military officer, former US Congressman Dave Weldon, writer Marielena Stuart and former Ruth's Chris Steakhouse CEO Craig Miller. For various reasons all but three of these had bowed out of the race by June of 2012.

Connie Mack, IV was seen as a strong early contender but in the Spring of 2011 announced he would not run and would back Senate President Haridopolos, who then appeared to be the front runner. In June, 2011, however, Haridopolos dropped out of the race, hounded by ethical questions and by criticism of his leadership during the 2011 legislative session. Republican Party leaders worried about what they perceived as a weak remaining field and urged Atwater to run, but he declined. Mack then reconsidered and jumped into the race in October, 2011 and Hasner and Miller dropped out in deference to Mack's statewide name recognition which was based very heavily on his father's reputation.

For a time, Mack's entry appeared to resolve the issue for Republicans. While a Quinnipiac Poll in November, 2011 showed 45% of potential Republican voters wanted "someone else or were not sure" about their choice, Mack got the most votes for a human and led by 32% to 9% over LeMieux. He also trailed Nelson by only 2%. The fact that Mack trailed Nelson, who had been a statewide political figure for over twenty years, by only two points lent credibility to his candidacy. Nevertheless, within five months doubts had set in regarding both Mack's and LeMieux's candidacies, Bill Nelson had opened a double digit lead over Mack and, in April, 2011, Jeff Atwater re-thought his entry into the race. After two days of reflection, he again declined to run, finally leaving the contest to Mack, LeMieux and the lightly regarded McCalister. The nature of the contest between these three is described below.

THE PRIMARY CAMPAIGN

The Republican Senate Primary: Background and Context

The senatorial primary in the Republican Party of Florida ultimately came down to a contest between two men who had gained the ability to compete for the position largely as a result of their associations with other men rather than on their own, individual accomplishments. (Three other candidates, Colonel Mike McCalister, former state representative Dave Weldon and Marielena Stuart persisted throughout the primary and in combination earned over 40% of the vote). George LeMieux was the protégé of former governor Charlie Crist, and Connie Mack, IV inherited his name and his political viability from his father, former US Senator Connie Mack, III. These associations had differential effects on the two candidates. Lemieux was forced to try to live down his ties to Crist, and Mack, IV had to try to live up to his father's reputation.

After graduation from Georgetown Law School, George LeMieux began his Florida political career as president of the Young Republicans in heavily Democratic Broward County where he invited a young state senator named Charlie Crist as a speaker. Subsequently, in 1998, the two cooperated on their own campaigns, LeMieux for the state legislature and for Crist for the Senate, and became friends. "Both men lost, but a bond was formed." (Bousquet, 2006) Four years later, LeMieux had taken over as Chair of the Broward County Republican Party and Crist had run successfully for Florida Attorney General and asked LeMieux to leave his job at a prominent local law firm in order to be chief of staff in the attorney general's office. Subsequently, Lemieux orchestrated Crist's election as Governor of Florida and became chief of staff in that office, where he was the moderately conservative Crist's closest confidant. He was in that position in 2010 when US Senator Mel Martinez announced that he would not complete his term in office and asked that a replacement be appointed as soon as possible to fill the remaining 16 months of his term.

At that point, Crist found himself in a politically tricky position. Faced with appointing someone to a job that he, himself, wanted, Crist turned to his longtime friend LeMieux. The appointment assured Crist that he would have an ally serving as the caretaker in the Senate, but exacerbated the emerging animosity between Crist and Tea Party conservatives in the Republican Party who wanted one of their own in the position. Marco Rubio, the conservative former Speaker of the Florida House who coveted the position and who won it by subsequently defeating Crist, said the governor had a "wealth of consistent and principled conservative candidates to choose from, all of whom would have been a reliable check and balance on the excesses of the Obama-Pelosi-Reid agenda" (Bennett. 2009). LeMieux's acceptance of the appointment, and his association with Crist, would come back to haunt him in 2012 when he sought the nomination to run against Nelson.

Like George LeMieux, Cornelius Harvey McGillicuddy, IV, popularly known as Connie Mack, IV came to political age in the shadow of another man, in this case his father. Cornelius Harvey McGillicuddy, III also known as Connie Mack, III represented Florida in the US Congress and in the US Senate over the years 1983 to 2001. Connie IV graduated from the University of Florida in 1993, became a marketing director and took a job as a special events coordinator for the Hooters restaurant/bar chain. In 2000, he ran for and was elected to the Florida State Legislature in the Atlantic coast beach town of Fort Lauderdale and was re-elected to the seat in 2002. In 2003, the incumbent Republican in US Congressional District 14 located one hundred forty miles across the state on the Gulf of Mexico in Ft. Myers announced he would not run for re-election. Mack, who had been raised in Ft. Myers when his father represented that district, sold his house in Ft. Lauderdale and moved to Ft. Myers in order to compete for the position where he had high name recognition. After winning an intense intra party primary fight in a heavily Republican district, he easily defeated his Democratic opponent and was elected to Congress, beginning in 2004. For the next eight years he served as a reliably conservative back bench Republican who made little policy or political impact. Perhaps his highest visibility came in 2007 when he married another member of Congress, from California. She was Mary Bono, the widow of the 1970's rock star Sonny Bono, the former husband of the legendary singer and Oscar award winning actress, Cher. His relative obscurity, combined with a variety of personal indiscretions, led to skepticism among Republicans that he could live up to the positive image willed to him by father's career.

The George LeMieux Campaign

Although George LeMieux began the race in the Republican primary as a former member of the US Senate, he also came into it bearing an association with Charlie Crist, the former Republican governor who had abandoned his party in 2010 in order to run for the US Senate as an Independent. This association severely limited LeMieux's appeal in a party that had only recently elected the extremely conservative, Tea Party backed, Marco Rubio and forced George to kick off his campaign by trying to portray himself as a conservative's conservative. He backed Representative Paul Ryan's conservative budget plan and said the US should not sign an agreement with Cuba to oversee oil spills in Cuba waters. He focused his attention on his record during the two years he served as the replacement for Mel Martinez and, like Rubio, began to call for changes to entitlement programs like Social Security and Medicare and to lobby for immediate cuts in federal spending. He also picked up an endorsement from former Mississippi Gov. Haley Barbour, who had briefly been a candidate for the Republican nomination for president.

Although he continued to push this message, LeMieux's campaign was never able to develop support among rank and file Republicans. In a Quinnipiac poll conducted in May, 2011 nearly two thirds of respondents (64%) chose "don't know" as the first option, with 14 % going to LeMieux (Quinnipiac Poll, 2011) and by early January, 2012 he had begun to fall well behind Congressman Connie Mack in polls of that party's likely voters. (Quinnipiac Poll, 2012)

As he began to lose ground to Mack, Senator LeMieux shifted his campaign away from extolling his own conservative bona fides and initiated an effort to diminish his opponent's character. In a May interview with MSNBC, he called Mack "the least qualified person to run for major office." (Graves, 2012; LeMieux 2012). He discussed Mack's involvement with Hooters, the restaurant/bar chain famous for their attention to female anatomy and ran a web video portraying the Congressman as a happy go-lucky, Joe College-type guy with "drunken bar fights, multiple road rage episodes, bounced checks and a failure to pay family support." (LeMieux 2012). The ad compared him unflatteringly to troubled actor Charlie Sheen and raised questions about his residency in Florida. LeMieux said Mack's "trying to run a campaign where people will mistake him for his father,' and that "Connie Mack can't win a character contest with Bill Nelson" (Graves).

Although LeMieux was joined in this portrayal of Mack by another candidate for the office,Tea Party favorite Mike McCalister, the message failed to gain traction and he could not shake his prior association with former governor Charlie Crist. By the middle of June, 2012, it became evident that his candidacy was simply not viable. He was behind Mack in fundraising, behind in endorsements by prominent political figures and behind in name identification. Facing these realities, he quit the race on June 20, saying "ahead of us in the polls, the Mack name enjoys widespread recognition that can only be matched with substantial advertising that our budget cannot support or the opportunity to debate on statewide television." (Caputo, 2012). Despite the invective he had launched against the Congressman, LeMieux did exit on a conciliatory note, saying "to continue would only hurt our (Republican) chances in the fall and that is not something that I will risk. Connie Mack will be the nominee. He has my support." (Ibid).

The Connie Mack Campaign

While Connie Mack, IV was initially regarded as a strong choice to run against Bill Nelson in 2012, he first declined the opportunity and lent his support instead to Florida Senate President Mike Haridopolis. Despite this reluctance, polls of Republican voters conducted in March, 2011 by Public Policy Polling showed him leading the race with 28 percent to 14 percent for George LeMieux and 14 percent for Haridopolis. When Haridopolus suddenly dropped his bid for the office in the summer of 2011, Mack changed his mind saying he had wanted someone to emerge who could defeat Bill Nelson and that did not happen. He officially announced his candidacy on Fox News' Sean Hannity Show on November 28. At this point, his lead in the polls had swelled to 32% to 9% over LeMieux, although 45% still preferred someone else/not sure. (Quinnipiac Poll, 2011)

In spite of (perhaps because of) Mack's prominence and visibility, his entry into the race was met with criticism from his Republican opponents as well as from Democrats. His GOP rivals attacked him on both policy grounds as well as on his family connections, while the Florida Democratic Party derided him for "relying more on his family's history than his lackluster record in Tallahassee and Washington or his vast professional experience planning parties for Hooters" (Derby, 2011).

With his entry into the race Mack quickly gained endorsements from major Florida Republicans, including former Governor Jeb Bush, Florida Attorney General Pam Bondi and Republican presidential candidate Mitt Romney. Soon after his announcement he also received word that he would receive a $1 million contribution from Las Vegas gambling magnate Sheldon Adelson, a Republican money giver who had supported Newt Gingrich in the Republican presidential primary (Caputo, 2012).

On the campaign trail, Mack had hoped to start by focusing on Bill Nelson, but the vigor of the attacks from his own party rivals forced him to spend initial weeks responding to them and especially to George LeMieux who he consistently tried to tie to Charlie Crist. Mack also tried to paint LeMieux as a liberal, arguing that he was one of two Republicans to vote for President Obama's jobs bill.

Despite the LeMieux distraction, Mack was immediately elevated to frontrunner status in the campaign, his fundraising totals began to elevate and he started to share the spotlight with the Republican presidential candidate. Refusing to participate in debates with his Republican competitors, he campaigned across the state with Mitt Romney, picking up valuable TV time and the aura of the favorite. Republican leaders in the US House also began to try to clear the field for him. They asked one of Mack's opponents, Adam Hasner, to run instead for Adam West's congressional seat when West vacated it to run for Congressman Tom Rooney's seat which had been vacated by Rooney in order to for him to run for another newly created seat. (Caputo, 2012)

Hasner's exit left only LeMieux and two other lightly regarded candidates in the race and Mack gradually shifted his campaign to focus on both LeMieux and Bill Nelson, the Democratic incumbent. His strategy was to label them both as too liberal for Florida. By April, 2012, Mack's campaign claimed that it was beating LeMieux in money, message and polls, and less than two months later, on June 22, LeMieux agreed and dropped out of the race. While both Mike McCalister and two other candidates stayed in the race until the bitter end, LeMieux's departure effectively ended the Republican primary and left Connie Mack as that party's candidate. He was officially declared the winner on August 14, winning 58.7% of the primary vote to 20.1% for Weldon, 13.9% for McCallister and 7.3% for Stuart. This modest victory was a portent of things to come in the general election.

THE US SENATE GENERAL ELECTION

The general election for the US Senate was to a considerable extent, a continuation of the contest that had been fought throughout the Republican primary. In that election the Connie Mack campaign sensed that he would defeat George LeMieux and tried to keep a focus on Bill Nelson while simultaneously holding off LeMieux. Nelson, on the other hand, capitalized on the attacks that LeMieux had launched against Mack and used them as the springboard for his own campaign.

As is usually the case in down ticket races, both candidacies were greatly influenced by their respective presidential candidates. Mack tied himself very tightly to Mitt Romney and joined in vigorous opposition to Barack Obama. As he said, "if Romney wins, I win." Bill Nelson recognized Obama's weakness in the state and tried to keep his distance, but could not completely disassociate himself from the President.

Connie Mack Campaign: General Strategy

In the aftermath of George LeMieux's withdrawal, Connie Mack was finally free to concentrate on his Democratic opponent, Bill Nelson. Arguing that "this election is the most important in our lifetime… and our very freedom, security, and prosperity hang in the balance" Mack immediately moved to buttress his conservative credentials, urging "all citizens of Florida who want less government, less taxing, less spending, and more freedom, to now join in our campaign" (Derby, 2012).

At its most general level, Mack attempted to turn the election into a referendum on the nation's economic performance under Barack Obama and to tie Bill Nelson to that performance. Republican Party officials recognized the importance of the presidential race to Mack's success. "It's all going to depend on the top of the ticket… if Romney gets to a four percentage point victory in Florida, there's a good chance that he'll bring Connie Mack with him." (Kennedy, 2012. Thus Mack's strategy was "keyed to catching a ride on Romney's coattails." To do this, Mack labeled Nelson and Obama as "lockstep liberals" who had supported economic policies that had "put our country on the road to Greece." He decried the American Recovery and Reinvestment Act of 2009 which put $787 billion into the nation's economy (and $13.4 billion into Florida's economy) as a "waste of money" and a "move to ignore the will of the American people." He called for repeal of the Affordable Care Act and he promoted his own economic proposal, called Mack's Penny Plan, that pledged to eliminate one penny out of every federal dollar spent each year, to cap spending at 18% of GDP, to balance the federal budget in less than a decade and to save taxpayers trillions over 10 years.

The Mack Air War

In pursuit of his objectives Congressman Mack mounted a multi-million dollar media campaign that was buttressed by an additional $11.4 million from 28 external groups such as the US Chamber of Commerce, American Crossroads, Americans for Prosperity, and Crossroads GPS (Open Secrets, 2012). In general, the television campaign was conducted on a "dual track" with the external groups typically providing the negative attacks and the Mack campaign promoting both negative and positive positions.

Ordinarily, political candidates open their campaigns with positive television and radio ads in which they "introduce" themselves by focusing on their own personal histories and characteristics. Connie Mack's first ad followed this strategy with a spot entitled "Freedom," a positive, patriotic theme that opened with the word superimposed over a waving American flag, followed by a shot of two astronauts planting a flag on the moon. Mack provides a voiceover, saying "Freedom, it's the core of all human progress." Almost simultaneously, came a different, more aggressively negative, spot entitled "Monkeying Around" that tied Senator Nelson to President Obama and claimed the president's stimulus bill, which Nelson supported, "wasted millions in taxpayer dollars on things like cocaine-addicted monkeys" (Politico, 2012). In a radio ad he also hit Nelson on his "stubborn refusal to accept the Keystone Pipeline System that would bring oil from Canada to various spots in the US (Ossowski, 2012). A number of external groups subsequently mimicked this negative strategy. American Crossroads spent $4 million on a negative ad that claimed that Nelson cast the "deciding vote" on the Affordable Care Act and the US Chamber of Commerce spent $3.8 million on a negative ad entitled "Obamacare" that also focused on Nelson's support for the Affordable Care Act. The argument in the US Chamber ads was that the ACA would reduce Medicaid spending by millions of dollars. Senator Nelson disputed the ad's accuracy and asked TV stations to pull it. (Holan, 2012). Freedom Works for America spent $2.8 million for ads that were both negative and positive and Feedom PAC spent $3.2 million on positive ads about Connie Mack.

The Mack Ground Game

Brett Doster, a long-time Republican field organizer was appointed to manage what political observers characterized as an anemic ground organization for Connie Mack. (Manjarres, 2012). In putting this component of the campaign into place, he relied on the Republican Party's highly regarded coordinated campaign for help. Mitt Romney's presidential campaign opened 47 offices around the state and all were components of the Republican National Committee's coordinated effort to boast Republican candidates up and down the ticket. The RNC saw this as an advantage since the local campaigns did not duplicate efforts. While the Mack campaign opened its own headquarters in his hometown of Bonita Springs, in large part, the candidate's field organization was managed from the RNC offices.

Mack exerted substantial effort to meet with and talk directly to Floridians. In October, 2012 his campaign announced that since January he had been on the road traveling more than 40,000 miles throughout the state. Some of this came via a series of week-long bus tours called Freedom Tours, which he conducted in September and October and concluded on Nov. 5 & 6 along with presidential candidate Mitt Romney.

Bill Nelson Campaign: General Strategy

In 2012, Bill Nelson had held elective office in Florida for over 30 years and had served in the Florida State Legislature, as a statewide elected official, in the US Congress and for two terms in the United States Senate. Nevertheless, he faced two substantial problems in his re-election bid: low approval ratings and a polarizing figure as the presidential candidate from his party.

Throughout his political career Bill Nelson had never been a widely popular official and his approval ratings had never been strong. Seven months before the 2012 election, these ratings were 36% approval and 32% disapproval and he had an "unusually low profile for a sitting two term Senator" (Public Policy Polling, April 18, 2012). He was viewed by Republicans as weak and as lucky in the opponents he had drawn in his previous senatorial races. He first won his seat in 2000 by defeating the "charisma challenged" Congressman Bill McCullom and subsequently was blessed with the controversial Katherine Harris as his opponent in 2006.

Nelson's second problem was that the Democrat at the top of the 2012 ticket, Barack Obama, was a polarizing figure in the state, one who also had low approval ratings, sometimes lower than those of Nelson. Given the effect of the presidential race on down ticket campaigns, Democrats feared (and Republicans hoped) that Obama's performance would pull Nelson down. Nelson's primary challenge was to minimize these weaknesses. He did so largely by playing to the strengths that had kept him in public office in Florida over much of his lifetime and by calling to attention the personal limitations of his opponent.

Part of Nelson's so-called "weakness" image stemmed from the efforts he had made throughout his career to cultivate an image as a noncontroversial figure who was distinct from national Democrats. He emphasized that "I'm a bipartisan consensus builder who gets things done" (Matthews, 2012). While this image may have appeared weak in the highly partisan atmosphere of Florida politics, it was not without advantages. As was pointed out by a former Democratic House Minority Leader, "Nelson is one of the few Democrats with a statewide identity and that really distinguishes him from every-one else, who is generally going to be tied to the national trend line... most strategists can envision a scenario in which Obama loses Florida but Nelson still wins" (Sullivan, 2012). Nelson relied upon this image throughout his campaign, "carefully nuancing his bonds to the While House. He cast him-self as a Democrat willing to work with Republicans on issues important to Floridians, like the oil-spill money, Everglades restoration and funding for the space program." (Kennedy, 2012). He also broke from the administration on parts of the Affordable Care Act and on the president's push to limit the Bush-era tax cuts to families making $250,000—Nelson would have raised the limit to $1 million. And he campaigned only once with the President, on the Sunday before Election Day.

The campaigns of both Bill Nelson and Connie Mack made efforts to distinguish themselves from each other on the basis of their positions on issues of importance to Floridians, but Nelson also attempted to paint Connie Mack as personally unfit for the position as US Senator. This line of attack had been initiated by George LeMieux in the Republican primary and was continued by Nelson throughout the general election. While it is impossible to ascertain the specific impact of individual components of a political cam-paign, many political pundits in Florida suggest that this early attack from his primary opponent and then from Bill Nelson "put Connie Mack on the defen-sive and that by the time he got to his feet, he was playing catch-up. And he never did." (Maxwell, 2012).

Bill Nelson Air War

The Nelson campaign expended $11.1 million on its 2012 media campaign. (Open Secrets, Florida. 2012) It adopted a dual track strategy featuring posi-tive ads such as "Bill Nelson . . . Fighting for Florida" as well as the negative attacks on Mack described above.

The "Bill Nelson...Fighting for Florida" ad described the Senator's early life and political career in Florida, his efforts to expose the lies of BP in the oil well disaster in the Gulf of Mexico, his fight against insurance companies for foreclosing on home owners during the financial crisis in the state and his long running battle for "faith, fairness and responsibility."

His negative ads began even before the general election was underway and built upon the ads George LeMieux had run against Mack in the primary portraying Mack as a "promoter for Hooters with a history of barroom brawls, altercations and road rage." Nelson also claimed that Mack didn't show up for work and tried to embarrass the Congressman for missing large numbers of votes in the House of Representatives. And finally, pointing to Mack's reliance on his father's name recognition, Nelson again capitalized on LeMieux's characterization of Mack as a "spoiled kid with a sense of entitlement" for the position.

THE OUTCOME OF THE SENATE RACE

At the onset of the 2012 race for the US Senate in Florida the contest "had the makings of a classic: vulnerable opponent in a big, colorful swing state opposed by a well-backed congressman with instant name recognition" (Liebovich. 2012). Connie Mack's entry into the race was "highly anticipated among Republicans as part of a multi-state strategy to win the four seats need to retake the Senate" (Klas and Sanders, 2012) and Republicans at the national level saw Florida as a prime pickoff opportunity. Al Cardenas, the former chair of the Florida Republican Party was quoted as saying "if you wanted to make a profile of the typical candidate who's been having problems in elections across the country, Bill [Nelson]would fit that profile" (Smith, 2012).

More objective observers never saw the potential for a Republican victory and it never became the dramatic contest it was often predicted to be. One observer thought that the two candidates "lulled each other to sleep" (Linkins, 2012) and others said that the race became "so boring, it's almost interesting," (Leibovich, 2012). The Nelson strategy was to attack Mack on a series of personal indiscretions, refuse face-to-face encounters and basically "hope no one notices that there is a Senate campaign going." Mack, on the other hand, never lived up to expectations. "When Connie Mack announced his candidacy, "it's almost like he sucked the air out of the race, but he wasn't able to sustain that. As more time went on, the reaction to him from people paying attention has become, 'Well, not so much.'" (Kennedy, 2012).

Chapter Eight

Explaining the Voter
in the Senate Election

According to some political watchers, the Senate seat held by Senator Bill Nelson was expected to stay in the column for the Democrats, though many believed it would be a tight race. While Sen. Nelson, the incumbent, was expected to win, the win was not expected to be a blowout. The dynamic of the campaign for Florida's senate seat is chronicled elsewhere in this study. This chapter, however, will focus on an analytical description of the popular vote for Senate and the social groups who supported each candidate. Based on exit polling data from the New York Time (2012). Senator Nelson won majorities of voters in nearly all key demographic groups (save white voters) in Florida.

GENERAL ELECTION RESULTS

Senator Bill Nelson won Florida's Senate seat with 55.2% of the vote compared to Connie Mack who won 42.2% of the vote. Bill Nelson received 4,523,451 votes compared to 3,458,267 votes for Connie Mack. Two independent candidates collectively received 208,168 votes. He carried the state winning with over 1 million votes more than his opponent.

County-by-County Results

Senator Nelson won 30 of the 67 Florida counties including those with the highest population density. He won majorities along the East Coast, the I-4 Corridor and Central Florida. Connie Mack, carried counties in the Panhandle and South -Central Florida which tend to be Republican strong holds.

Mack and Nelson both carried counties in North Florida but Mack won more counties in North Florida than did Senator Nelson. It is also interesting to note that Senator Nelson won more counties than did President Obama suggesting that the coattail effect from Romney did not carry over to help Connie Mack. Senator Nelson was able to win in counties where Obama wasn't able to secure victories.

When examining the voting behavior of key demographic constituencies, Senator Nelson was able to win majorities in every demographic group necessary to put together a winning election. He won a majority of men, women, black and Hispanic voters, and all age groups, while Connie Mack was only able to win a majority of white voters.

Sex

Senator Nelson won 51% of male voters and 59% of female voters.

Race and Ethnicity

Senator Nelson won 96% of Black voters while his opponent Connie Mack won 52% of the white vote.

Age

Senator Nelson won all four age groups. Among 18–29 year olds he captured 65% of the vote; 40–44 year olds 57% of the vote; 45–64 year olds 54% of the vote; and those 65+, 50% of the vote.

SUMMARY OF KEY DEMOGRAPHIC GROUPS

While Senator Bill Nelson won majorities among key constituencies; the change from 2008 is especially noteworthy. Republicans gained in nearly every group discussed except for black and Hispanic voters. This should signal a bright spot for Republicans and an area of concern for Democrats.

Education

Senator Nelson ran the table as well when it came to education. Among those with no college degree he had 56% of the vote, among those with some college 53% of the vote, among college grads 60% of the vote, and among post graduates 68% of the vote.

Table 8.1. County by County Results: US Senate Election in Florida

United States Senator County	Connie Mack (REP)	Bill Nelson (DEM)	Bill Gaylor (NPA)	Chris Borgia (NPA)
Alachua	41,834	72,439	1,367	1,088
Baker	6,940	3,884	216	99
Bay	47,530	28,480	1,600	883
Bradford	6,605	4,529	233	93
Brevard	127,177	142,072	6,429	3,195
Broward	212,803	510,987	5,382	4,789
Calhoun	3,035	2,737	179	81
Charlotte	42,168	37,617	2,185	1,023
Citrus	35,112	34,574	1,821	1,124
Clay	59,584	30,999	1,996	1,146
Collier	85,194	54,784	2,211	1,325
Columbia	15,055	10,725	583	236
Desoto	4,661	4,637	242	106
Dixie	3,755	2,724	174	84
Duval	177,958	211,493	6,979	4,801
Escambia	76,893	64,793	1,930	1,236
Flagler	22,029	25,430	904	555
Franklin	2,621	2,622	82	51
Gadsden	5,429	16,442	201	113
Gilchrist	4,692	2,783	158	80
Glades	1,903	1,823	93	47
Gulf	3,675	3,123	166	63
Hamilton	2,554	2,561	99	46
Hardee	3,611	3,101	223	102
Hendry	4,632	5,002	204	129
Hernando	34,902	43,691	1,985	1,183
Highlands	20,354	19,110	1,008	500
Hillsborough	203,595	308,910	7,741	5,614
Holmes	5,589	2,236	209	106
Indian River	36,551	29,563	1,265	879
Jackson	10,624	9,574	316	168
Jefferson	2,941	4,549	98	53
Lafayette	2,130	1,119	57	39
Lake	71,463	69,791	3,418	1,602
Lee	133,746	117,773	5,367	2,902
Leon	46,379	94,323	1,617	1,215
Levy	9,557	7,833	433	176
Liberty	1,539	1,587	69	42

Madison	3,545	4,763	134	78
Manatee	70,721	73,985	3,259	1,687
Marion	75,967	76,930	3,452	1,774
Martin	40,901	33,767	982	568
Miami-Dade	292,757	523,461	5,560	6,180
Monroe	17,013	19,506	467	300
Nassau	24,773	13,313	780	475
Okaloosa	61,796	27,098	2,126	1,155
Okeechobee	5,554	5,972	254	160
Orange	153,241	282,090	5,578	3,384
Osceola	32,331	69,690	1,750	1,114
Palm Beach	198,238	362,499	4,724	3,603
Pasco	87,620	111,764	4,930	3,467
Pinellas	167,380	263,427	8,305	6,318
Polk	107,393	126,722	4,860	2,690
Putnam	14,942	14,560	808	419
Santa Rosa	50,772	21,893	1,516	884
Sarasota	93,502	102,569	3,311	1,983
Seminole	90,179	106,371	2,863	2,232
St. Johns	66,626	41,171	2,218	1,498
St. Lucie	45,989	70,179	1,557	1,218
Sumter	34,058	23,410	1,183	559
Suwannee	10,480	6,277	430	169
Taylor	4,802	3,914	175	81
Union	3,070	2,057	93	52
Volusia	95,927	126,302	4,275	2,487
Wakulla	7,098	6,700	352	187
Walton	18,433	8,480	636	280
Washington	6,339	4,161	261	113
Total	3,458,267	4,523,451	126,079	82,089
% Votes	42.2%	55.2%	1.5%	1.0%

Income

Across all income categories, Bill Nelson swept voters. He captured 66% of those making less than $30K a year, 61% of those earning between$ 30K and$ 49.9K, 50% of those earning $50K or more, and he tied his challenger among those making $100K or more. This is no small feat for a Democrat.

City vs. Suburbs

Like the analysis of Presidential voting behavior in an earlier chapter, Senator Nelson's votes mirror that of President Obama. Senator Nelson won the majority of voters in mid-sized cities (61% of the vote) and the suburbs (56%

Table 8.2.   Social Characteristics of Florida Voters and the US Senate Vote

	Florida	Percent Change from 2008 in FLORIDA
Sex	51% Nelson	+8% Republican
Male	59% Nelson	+3% Republican
Female		
Race and Ethnicity	52% Mack	+9% Republican
White	90% Nelson	Unchanged
Black	59% Nelson	+1% Democrat
Hispanic	NA	
Asian		
Age	65% Nelson	+2% Republican
18-29	57% Nelson	+4% Republican
30-44	54% Nelson	+7% Republican
45-64	50% Nelson	+8% Republilcan
65+		

of the vote) while his opponent Connie Mack won in big cities (50% of the vote) and small cities (55%) of the vote.

Political Party and Ideology

Like President Obama, Senator Nelson maintained the support of his party and Liberals, while Connie Mack held support of Republicans and Conservatives. Among Independents, Senator Nelson won 57% of the vote compared to 40% won by Connie Mack. Moderates voted 61% in favor of Bill Nelson, compared to 37% who voted for Connie Mack.

The Economy

The NYT Exit Poll asked about the economy. Among those who believed the economy was excellent or good 86% voted for Bill Nelson and among those who believed the economy was not so good or poor, 55% voted for Connie Mack.

SUMMARY

Though Senator Bill Nelson won by a large margin and among nearly all the various demographic groups that traditionally support Democratic candidates and among groups that often favor Republicans (those making over $50k a year and those 65 years of age and older). The pattern may be one of caution for Democrats as they look at the gains made by the Republican party across all demographic areas. In nearly every group, Republicans made gains.

Table 8.3.   Other Characteristics of Florida Voters and the US Senate Vote

	Florida	Percent Change from 2008 in FLORIDA
Education:	56% Nelson	NA
No college	53% Nelson	+2% Republican
Some college	52% Mack	+6% Republican
College	57% Nelson	+6% Republican
Postgrad		
Income:	66% Nelson	Unchanged
Under 30K	61% Nelson	Unchanged
30-49.9K	50% Nelson	+7% Republican
50k or more	49% TIED	NA
100K or more		
City v. Suburb:	50% Mack	+3% Republican
Big city	61% Nelson	+5% Republican
Mid-size city	55% Mack	+5% Republican
Small city	56% Nelson	+5% Republican
Suburbs		
Ideology:	88% Nelson	+1% Republican
Liberal	61% Nelson	+8% Republican
Moderate	73% Mack	+6% Republican
Conservative		
Political Party:	92% Nelson	+3% Republican
Democrat	83% Mack	+8% Republican
Republican	57% Nelson	+12 Republican
Independent		
The Economy is:	86% Nelson	NA
Excellent/good	55% Mack	NA
Not so good/poor		

While this should cause angst for Democrats, Republicans should be encouraged by the gains that were made in 2012 compared to 2008, despite the loss of Connie Mack to Senator Bill Nelson.

III

The Race for Congress

Chapter Nine

The Campaign for Congress

INTRODUCTION

The Congressional campaigns in Florida in 2012 were the first such elections conducted after the 2011 reapportionment when Florida was awarded two additional Congressional seats and when the boundaries of all the now 27 districts were redrawn by the Florida State Legislature. The boundaries in 2011 were drawn in compliance with the Fair Districts constitutional amendment adopted by Floridians in 2010. This amendment was designed to remediate the influence of partisan politics in setting district boundaries and was an effort to prevent the state legislature from utilizing its control over the reapportionment process to prejudice legislative boundaries in favor of the majority party. The new boundaries released in 2011 were immediately challenged as violating the Fair Districts amendment, but they set the parameters of the 2012 election, even as the challenge wound its way through the courts. And these parameters gave the Republicans the advantage. In a state in which registered Democrats outnumber registered Republicans by 4.7 million to 4.2 million and where 44.7% of residents identified with the Democratic Party as opposed to 40.2% with the Republicans, the Democrats were able to win 8 congressional seats as compared to 19 for the Republicans in an election year in which the Democratic president won the state's 29 electoral votes. A brief discussion of the races in each of the state's 27 congressional districts is provided below.

District 1

The First Congressional District is the westernmost of Florida's congressional districts, bordering Alabama. Made up of five counties, the 2012 district changed very little after reapportionment and remains one of the most conservative, and least racially diverse, districts in the nation. In 2012 it had R+21 rating on Cook's voting index. In 2012, the incumbent was Republican Jeff Miller who had represented the district since 2001 after a special election due to the resignation of another Republican, Joe Scarborough. Miller, one of the staunchest conservatives in the House began his career in the Florida House of Representatives and had been a deputy sheriff. The Democratic candidate was Jim Bryan, the owner of a towing business who had previously been a professional soldier; a former army paratrooper with 3 combat tours in Vietnam and two purple hearts for combat wounds. Miller was easily re-elected with 69.6% to Bryan's 27.1%.

District 2

Congressional District 2 is located in the middle of Florida's panhandle and abuts Georgia on the north. Reapportionment re-organized the district's geography substantially, with only modest effects on partisanship. It remained largely rural, with 12 entire counties and large parts of two others. After reapportionment in 2011, voter registration showed 52% Democrat and 32% Republican, but a R+3 Cook PVI. In 2010, voter registration was 60.6% Democratic and 39.4% Republican and the PVI was R+6. A Republican victory in both 2010 and 2012 suggested that many of the district's Democrats had left that Party without changing their registration.

The 2010 race in Congressional District 2 had been one of the most competitive and most aggressive in the nation. It pitted a long-time "Blue Dog" Democrat incumbent, Alan Boyd, against an extremely conservative "Tea Party" Republican, Steve Sutherland, an undertaker from Bay County who had the financial backing of numerous conservative PACs as well as the Republican National Committee. Buoyed by the wave of discontent with President Obama and Boyd's support of the Affordable Care Act, Sutherland won the race easily, by a margin of 53.6% to 41.4%.

As a first term incumbent in a district long held by Democrats, in 2012 Southerland was a prime target for the Democratic National Committee and Florida Democrats and after a highly competitive primary, the Democrats selected Al Lawson, an African American who had represented parts of the district in both the Florida House of Representatives and the state Senate.

In a campaign in which the opponents disagreed on virtually every issue in play and in which external groups played a major role, Sutherland won by 52.7% to 47.3%. This outcome left some ambiguity about the political nature of the district. While it is competitive, Republicans are feeling increasingly secure but Democrats are still thinking it is winnable.

District 3

This district also borders the state of Georgia, but encompasses land east of District 2. The district is composed of Gainesville and Alachua County, which makes up over 30% of the total population as well as all of 8 other entire counties and parts of three more. It stretches from the Georgia border in the North to the coast of the Gulf of Mexico in the South. The district contested in 2012 was completely different from that contested in 2010. It drew population from the old Second, Fourth, Fifth and Sixth districts, a total of 13 counties. Although voter registration was equally split between Democrats and Republicans, the district had an R+13 rating from Cook's political index and an incumbent Republican from part of the old 6th district, Cliff Stearns. Stearns had his hometown of Ocala drawn into the new 11th District, but opted to seek re-election in the new 3rd which contained more than two thirds of his former district.

As is usually the case in a new, safe, district, a number of challengers arose to take on Stearns in the Republican primary. They included a Florida State Senator, the Clay County Clerk of Court and a large animal veterinarian from Gainesville. Stearns, a 12 term congressman raised over 2 million dollars, enhanced his profile by conducting investigations into Planned Parenthood and government loans to the failed energy company Solyndra, but campaigned only moderately. At the end of his campaign he was sitting on more than $2 million and lost to the veterinarian, Ted Yoho, who was backed by the Tea Party and whose campaign accused Stearns of being a career politician and portrayed him as a pig feeding from a trough. Yoho also suggested that voting should be limited to property owners and called early voting a travesty. (Strauss, 2014). Yoho won 11 of the district's 13 counties and beat Stearns by 829 votes. He went on to defeat Democrat J.R. Gailot, a Haitian making his first foray into public office by 65% to 32% in the general election.

District 4

District Four is located in the north eastern corner of Florida, abutting Georgia and fronting on the Atlantic Ocean. It shrank considerably in geographical size after the 2011 reapportionment (from 6 whole counties and portions of 3 others) and now contains two whole counties (Baker and Nassau) and part of Duval, almost entirely the beach communities on the Atlantic Coast. Jacksonville (Duval County) makes up about 85% of the district, but it is the white suburbs of Jacksonville. Republicans make up 58.8% of the district and it carries a Cook PVI of R+19.

The incumbent Republican in old District 4 was Ander Crenshaw, who had represented the district for the previous 14 years. He faced minimal competition in the 2012 Republican primary for the seat in the new district and the Democrats endorsed no candidate in the general election. Jim Klauder who ran with no party affiliation received 23.9% of the vote in that election.

District 5

The Fifth District was formerly Florida's 3rd district, created as a "majority minority" district in 2000 and completely changed in the 2011 reapportionment. In the decade prior to 2011, District 3 was located on the western coast of Florida, bordering the Gulf of Mexico. The new 5th District is a long, narrow one located in inland Florida. It includes parts of eight counties and no whole ones. Duval and Orange counties make up about 80% of the population total and African Americans make up 52% of that population. The District is facing close scrutiny in the lawsuit over the manner in which districts were re-drawn in the 2011 reapportionment.

The incumbent in District 3 was Corrine Brown who had held the seat since 1992. Given the nature of her district, Brown had rarely had strong opposition from Republicans and often ran unopposed. Even though the new district of 2012 had a D+21 PVI, the Republicans did run a candidate, LeAnne Kolb, founder of AFR Christian Karate and a first time office seeker who favored the Fair Tax, US withdrawal from the UN and repeal of the Affordable Care Act. Brown won by 70.8% to 26.3% for Kolb.

District 6

This District also underwent significant change in the 2011 reapportionment. Redistricting completely shifted its geographical region and the new district contained none of its previous counties. The "old" district had a R+8 PVI. The new district had an R+6 rating and two Republican incumbents from separate parts of the old district. One, Republican Cliff Stearns, was thrown into District 3 by the reapportionment. Another incumbent from a portion of the District, Republican John Mica, opted to run in the new 7th District, leaving new District 6, composed of all of Flagler and St. Johns Counties and portions of Putnam and Volusia, as an open seat in the election of 2012.

The new district had a slightly larger number of registered Republicans than Democrats and a PVI of R+6. It thus attracted six candidates to the Republican primary, including State Representative Fred Costello, Beverly Slough, the Chair of the St. John's County School Board, and Ron DeSantis, an attorney from Ponte Vedra Beach who had written a book about conservative principles that earned him the embrace of the Tea Party and the endorsement of numerous professional conservatives from around the nation, including Maricopa County, NM, Sheriff Joe Arpaio, businessman Donald Trump and former US Ambassador John Bolton.

DeSantis easily won his party primary, capturing 39% of the total vote compared to 23% for the next highest vote getter, State Representative Costello. In the general election, DeSantis raised more than four times the money as did his opponent, Democrat Heather Beaven and won by 57.2% to 42.8%.

District 7

District 7 is located near the middle of Florida and contains 91% of the residents of Orange County and smaller percentages of Seminole and Volusia counties. It is a dramatically different district than it was in its previous incarnation and is now a combination of the old Eighth and Twenty Forth districts. Voter registration in the new District was 39.5% Republican, 34.0% Democrat and 25.2% NPA. In 2012 it had an R+5 PVI.

The important race in this campaign took place in the Republican primary where two incumbent Congressmen, John Mica, a mainstream conservative and Sandy Adams, a Tea Party favorite, faced off. Mica had previously represented much of what became the new 6th District while Adams represented the old 24th District. About 50% of her old district was brought into the new one.

As the campaign developed, it turned into one of the nastiest of the year, with both sides accusing the other of lying and committing various unethical acts. Mika cast the race as a contest between a long time public servant with a proven conservative record and an inexperienced freshman member with minimal success serving the causes she espoused in the campaign. Adams pointed to her endorsements from Sarah Palin, Representative Alan West and the Tea Party Express to frame the race as one between "true" conservatives and those who were Republicans in name only. In the end, Mica nearly doubled the amount of money raised by Adams ($1.6 million to $941,902) and defeated her by 61.2% of the vote to 38.8%.

In the general election Mica defeated outmanned Democrat Jason Kendall, a Soil and Water Conservation Supervisor from Seminole County, by 58.7% to 41.3% of the vote.

District 8

The new District 8 was created from the former 15th and 24th Districts and included Brevard, Indian River and a small part of Orange Counties. A predominantly Republican district, it had 44.2% registered Republicans, 33.5% Democrats and a PVI of R+8. Upon the creation of the new district, the incumbent congressman from the 15th, Republican Bill Posey, announced his candidacy and faced no primary opposition. In the general election the Democrats ran Shannon Roberts, a business consultant with previous experience working for NASA and the federal government. She was also a member of the city council in Cape Canaveral, Fl.

Posey, perhaps best known for his sponsorship in Congress of the "birther bill" that challenged the legality of President Obama's birthplace, raised more than 100 times the money as did Roberts (in July of 2012 his total was $837,931 compared to $6,759 for Roberts) and won the election by 58.9% to 37.5%.

District 9

The 9th congressional district was completely relocated in the 2011 reapportionment. Previously coastal and heavily populated, the new Ninth looked more like the old 12th and 15th. It moved inland and now includes part of Orange (Orlando) and all of rural Polk and Osceola Counties. It also left behind the incumbent Republican, Gus Bilirakis, who was moved to the new 12th District. The new District contains only 31% of Orange County, but that county makes up over 50% of the total population. The demographic composition of the district also changed substantially. The old district had a population of 56.3% African American and 59.5% white. The new district was composed of 44.1% Hispanics, 11.8% African American and 39.5% white. Democrats hold a sizeable advantage in voter registration, with 42.2% to 27.4% for Republicans. The PVI in 2012 was D+4.

With no incumbent and a Democratic edge, the first candidate to announce was Alan Grayson, a Democrat from Windermere, who had lost a seat in Congress in 2010 in the former District 8. A personally wealthy, flamboyantly liberal Democrat, Grayson faced one major hurdle, he was not Puerto Rican and the new district was heavily so. However, anticipating the reapportionment, Grayson had carefully wooed the area's Puerto Rican community while in the 8th District and after his defeat continued his contacts with the group. When the 2012 race began, he and a liberal independent PAC quietly ran over $100,000 in negative ads in the Republican primary against the one Republican Hispanic who had enough name recognition to challenge him, knocking him out of the race and leaving Todd Long, a conservative radio host who had failed in earlier attempts to get elected to Congress. Given Grayson's financial resources and the nature of the district, conservative external groups who had backed Grayson's opponent in 2010, backed away from Long. He was unable to raise enough money to compete and by October "was reduced to waving signs at intersections" (Pinsky. 2013).

District 10

The composition of District 10 was changed substantially in the 2011 reapportionment plan. Once a small territory on the coast, the new district was relocated in the middle of the state, was expanded in geographical size and encompassed parts of the old 8th and 12th Districts. In this new district, Republicans held a voter registration advantage over Democrats by 174,166 to 153,040 and The PVI was R+7.

Despite the Republican-lean of the District, the race in the general election was hard-fought and close. It attracted big money from outside groups supporting the two candidates, Daniel Webster the incumbent Republican and Val Demings the Democrat, but mostly aimed at the Republican. The Democratic Congressional Campaign Committee also spent $1.5 million on behalf of the Democratic candidate.

Both of the candidates were well-known in the District—Webster had been the Speaker of the Florida House and the Majority Leader in the State Senate in addition to being the incumbent Congressman. Demings, an African American, had been the City of Orlando's first female Chief of Police and her husband was the Sheriff of Orange County.

Webster, a quiet campaigner, stuck to the message he had preached throughout his political career, the Federal budget is out of control and should be reined in. Demings generally stuck to the Democratic Party's platform except in the District's conservative areas where she spoke often about her willingness to go against her party.

Although Demings and her supporters far outspent Webster, the District favors Republicans and Webster was a widely known and well-respected official. He won the race by 51.9% to 48.1%.

District 11

In its 2010 incarnation, District 11 was made up mostly of Tampa, its suburbs and southeastern Hillsborough County. It also included neighborhoods in Pinellas County and in Bradenton in Manatee County. The "new" District 11 was completely shifted and after the 2011 reapportionment was made up of all of Citrus and Hernado Counties as well as parts of Lake, Marion, and Sumter. In 2012 the district was strongly Republican and carried an R+8 PVI.

The Republican candidate in the race was the incumbent from the former 5th District, Richard Nugent who was seeking his first re-election after serving as sheriff of Hernando County. Nugent called himself a "strong conservative."

The Democrats nominated David Werder, a disabled former truck driver who had made a name for himself as a protestor/flag pole sitter (sat on a pole for 439 days to protest high gas prices), and who had been unsuccessfully running for office for years at the federal and local levels. He was anti-tax and believed that the federal government should run its own hospitals to provide healthcare to all. Nugent was returned to Congress by a margin of 64.5% to 35.5% for Werder.

District 12

The 12th District is located on the western edge of Florida and is comprised primarily of Pasco County, with small portions of Hillsboro and Pinellas Counties. In reapportionment it drew upon the old 9th and 5th Districts. In 2012 it had a PVI of R+6.

The incumbent in the 9th was Gus Bilirakis who had succeeded his father in the 2006 race and who became the Republican candidate without primary opposition. His main priorities included controlling government spending, creating jobs for middle class Americans, operating smaller and smarter government, and lowering taxes.

The Democrats nominated Jonathan Snow, a first time candidate for office who was a photo technician at Walgreens. Issues included cutting waste and fraud, eliminate tax loopholes and havens, strengthen Medicare by allowing all Americans to buy into it and allow negotiating with pharmaceutical manufacturers, passing the DREAM act and reducing immigration backlog.

Conducting a vastly more expensive and professional campaign than Snow, Bilirakis won by 62.5% to 32.9% of the vote.

District 13

In the aftermath of the 2011 reapportionment process, the 13th Congressional District was composed of the western portion of the Tampa Bay area, including all but the southern tip of the peninsula. It more closely resembled the 10th District rather than the former 13th because of re-numbering in the redistricting process. Both the 13th and the previous 10th are entirely within Pinellas County. The thirteenth District is very evenly divided in terms of partisanship with 38.1% registered as Republicans, 35.1 Democratic and 22.5 NPA. In 2012, the District carried an R+1 PVI.

The incumbent in the District was Bill Young who had represented this area of Florida in Congress for 42 years and was the senior Republican in Congress. His Democratic opponent, Jessica Ehrlich, was a business woman working in international business and finance in New York who felt compelled to work in public policy after surviving the terrorist attack on 9/11. She then got her law degree, worked in a staff position in Congress and as a clerk to the Chief Judge of the US Federal Court for Middle Florida in Tampa. This was her first time running for public office.

Young raised more than twice the money as did Ehrlich and called upon his long record of "bringing home the bacon" to the district to win the election by 57.6% of the vote to Ehrlich's 42.4%.

District 14

Florida's 14th Congressional District is made up of the eastern and southern regions of the Tampa Bay area, midway along Florida's Atlantic coast. As a consequence of redistricting in 2011, the new 14th represented an entirely different geographic area than did its earlier version, looking more like the old 11th District. The new 14th District contained over 87% of the previous 11th District, along with portions of the old 10th and 9th. This rearrangement gave the new 14th District half of Hillsborough County and 10% of Pinellas. A racially diverse district, the 14th had 49% registered Democrats, 25% registered Republicans and 26% registered unaffiliated. In 2012 the PVI was D+11.

The incumbent in the old 11th District was Democrat Kathy Castor who was first elected in 2006 and she was unopposed as the Democratic candidate in the 14th in 2012. In the general election she was challenged by Evelio "EJ" Otero, a former Air Force colonel who had worked as a military and political commentator and intelligence consultant. Castor raised more than 10 times the money as did Otero and was easily re-elected, by a margin of 70.3% to 29.7%.

District 15

Unlike its previous incarnation, the new 15th Congressional District is located in inland Florida and draws its population from only two counties, Hillsborough and Polk. It lost Brevard, Indian River and Osceola counties in reapportionment and resembled the old 12th District more than the old 15th. A racially homogenous district, the 15th is relatively equal in partisanship. Forty percent of the registered voters are Republican, 39.1% are Democrats and 20.8% are unaffiliated. It had a PVI of R+8 in 2012 and a Republican incumbent from the old 12th District, Dennis Ross. Ross was unchallenged in the Republican primary and ran unopposed in the general election.

District 16

The 16th District of Florida was changed very substantially from its predecessor. It went from a medium-sized, predominantly inland district to a small coastal one. It drew heavily from old districts 11 and 13. A demographically homogenous district (83.5% white), its racial composition is significantly different from Florida as a whole. Republicans outnumbered Democrats by 45% to 33% and the District carried a PVI of R+5.

The Republican candidate in 2012 was Vern Buchanan who held the 13th District seat before reapportionment and was elected to that seat in a tightly contested and highly controversial race in 2006. In that race, Mr. Buchanan was victorious over the Democrat by a margin of fewer than 400 votes and a malfunction in the electronic voting machine invalidated 14,000 votes. A post-election investigation showed that had these ballots been counted, Mr. Buchanan would have lost by about 3,000 votes. (Ash, Arlene and Lampeti, 2008).

With the 2011 reapportionment, they thought they had a good opportunity and they found a good candidate to pursue it. He was Keith Fitzgerald, a professor of political science at Florida's New College who had represented the area in the Florida House of Representatives for four years, losing in the Republican "wave" election of 2010.

In 2012, Mr. Fitzgerald raised $1.4 million and made allegations about Mr. Buchanan's alleged illegal campaign contributions the center of his campaign. Mr. Buchanan refuted the charges and based his campaign on his opposition to the Democratic administration in Washington. In a district that favors the Republicans, his efforts were successful and he won by 53.6% to 43.4% of the vote.

District 17

The 17th Congressional District in Florida underwent a huge change in the 2011 reapportionment. Located in the middle of the state, it encompasses the entirety of 6 counties and parts of three others. It also includes portions of five other former congressional districts, the 16th, the 12th, the 14th, the 13th and the 9th.

In the 2012 race, the incumbent was Republican Tom Rooney who had represented the 16th District since 2008 and did not live in the 17th when elected. Heir to a famous Pennsylvania family who owned the Pittsburgh Steelers, Rooney had been raised in Florida and served in the US Army JAG corps and taught at West Point prior to becoming a candidate for political office. His campaign platform included reforming the tax code, eliminating costly and unnecessary regulations, and promoting American energy production, including offshore drilling. He was also opposed to the Affordable Care Act.

Rooney's opponent was Democrat Will Bronson, a retired Delta Airlines pilot who had run for Congress as a Republican in both Massachusetts and Georgia. Heavily outspent, Bronson lost to Rooney by 41.4% to 58.6% of the vote.

District 18

The 18th congressional district created in 2011 bore no resemblance to the previous District of this number. The new district was a combination of the old 16th, 19th, 22nd, and 23rd Districts. It is located on the Eastern border of the state and includes the counties of Martin, St. Lucié, and the northern part of Palm Beach. A very homogenous District, it is 82% Caucasian, 8% African American and 7% Hispanic. Republicans register about 10,000 more voters than do Democrats and the PVI wasR+1.

In the aftermath of the 2011 reapportionment, Republican incumbents in Central Florida found themselves in overlapping districts. For example, Representative Tom Rooney, who had represented a section of District 16 (which became part of the new 18) elected to run in new District 17 instead of new District 18, allowing Allen West who had represented District 22, another part of the new District 18 to run as an incumbent in that District. The race for this seat became one of the most highly publicized congressional campaigns in the nation in 2012.

In 2010, Allen West had emerged from political nowhere to become a Tea Party star by adopting rhetoric "in which every sentence is a proxy war in the larger struggle between patriots and the people in the world that just have to have their butts kicked." (Gibbs 2012). He said, "there are those who will hate your own country, America, regardless of the self-evident truths. To you I say that life just does not get any better than the 'Land of the all night IHop' and if you truly hate America so much, you are also free to find another home. There is surely an illegal immigrant who will be happy in yours." (Isenstadt. 2012) He called fellow member of Congress Debbie Wasserman Schultz "vile, unprofessional and despicable," said President Obama was "probably the dumbest person walking around in America right now," and said House Minority Leader and other Democrats should "get the hell out of the United States of America."(Ibid) He raised more than $5 million for his campaign and defeated incumbent Democrat Ron Klein by a margin of 8.8%.

In the 2012 race West was pitted against Patrick Murphy, a political newcomer who had been a Republican up until 2011. In this race, West continued the rhetoric that won him support among conservatives such as Sarah Palin, Ted Nugent and Glen Beck. He raised an astonishing 19 million dollars and continued the rhetoric that had made him famous. During the campaign West tried to tear down Murphy in highly personal terms rather than presenting his compelling life story. Republican campaign consultants claimed that "this was a Congressional operation run amuck."

For his part, Murphy raised nearly $5 million for his campaign and branded himself as a nonpartisan who would be a quiet, get-it-done member of Congress. He secured an important endorsement from Republican sheriff Bob Crowder who had lost to West in the Republican primary and defeated

West by 50.3% to 49.7% of the vote. Although West contested the outcome, a re-count improved Murphy's margin of victory and the Democrats picked up a Republican seat in Congress. In the aftermath of the campaign, former Congressman Ron Klein, whom West had defeated in 2010, said "West beat himself." (Ibid)

District 19

The 19th District that emerged out of the 2011 reapportionment was located on the south western coast of Florida and was composed primarily of territory previously included in the old 14th District and a very small portion of the old 25th. There were two counties in the District, Collier and Lee. A solid Republican district, the PVI in 2012 was R+11 and Republican registrants outnumbered Democrats by 47.1% to 27.4%, with 22% indicating no partisan affiliation.

The incumbent in District 19 was Connie Mack, III who resigned the seat on Nov. 28, 2011 to run for the US Senate against Democrat Bill Nelson. Mack's resignation left vacant a heavily Republican seat and invited an intra-party battle that featured several high visibility Republican candidates. They included Chauncey Goss, the son of Porter Goss who had represented the District for more than15 years before Mack, Gary Aubuchon who served six years in the state legislature and was chair of that body's Rules and Calendar Committee, Paige Kreegel who was serving his fourth term in the state House and political newcomers Byron Donalds and Trey Radel.

Radel came to South Florida in 2003 for a job with Naples television station WINK-TV. In 2009, he took over a conservative talk show on a radio station owned by WINK and began a career that established him as a major conservative voice in southwest Florida. "The jump from there to politics felt like a calling, Radel said." (Staats, 2012).

Radel's tenure on WINK provided him instant name recognition and Goss said his internal polling showed that Radel had a dedicated base and was at the top of the heap through much of the campaign. (Ibid) As the frontrunner, Radel was the focus of attention in the campaign and attracted attacks from ads from several opponents that "portrayed him as a laughing goof and invoked scandals over his (private) company's buying and selling of sexy Latino website names and over what his opponents called his campaign's dirty tricks of buying website names his opponents likely would have used for their own campaigns." (Ibid) His wife, a popular TV news anchor, defended him in an effective TV ad and he went on to beat his nearest rival by 8%.

Radel's Democratic opponent in the general election was Jim Roach, a decorated Vietnam veteran and former GM engineer who owned a technology consulting company. Facing a heavily Republican electorate and an opponent who outspent him by $1.1 million to $86,000, Roach lost to Radel by 62% to 35%.

District 20

District 20 is one of three "minority majority" districts created in Florida under court order to enhance the ability of racial minorities to elect candidates of their own race to public office. Both the geography and the demography of the district changed in the 2011 reapportionment, but it sustained its previous heavily minority status. Geographically, the district is located in the center of the state and includes Palm Beach, Broward and Hendry Counties. The district is not contiguous. During the 2011 reapportionment, the white population decreased from 36.7% to 29.5%, the African American population increased from 46.7% to 52.6% and the Hispanic population increased from 12.6% to 17.7%. Registered Democrats outnumbered registered Republicans by 82% to 18%. The PVI was D+28.

The incumbent in District 20 was Alcee Hastings, the first African American federal judge in Florida. A strong advocate of the rights of minorities, women, children and immigrants, Hastings had held the seat since 1992. His opponent in 2012 was Terry Long, founder of Operation Rescue, an anti-abortion advocacy group, and one of America's best known pro-life leaders. Long ran without party affiliation and was defeated by 87.9% of the vote to 12.1%.

District 21

The 21st District lies on the eastern edge of Florida and includes territory from only two counties, Broward and Palm Beach. The new district is quite different from its previous incarnation and drew heavily from the old 19th and 22nd Districts. During reapportionment, the demographic composition of the district changed from 78% white to 62% white, and the Hispanic population increased from 12.1% to 19.2. African Americans made up 10.6% of the population. Democrats outnumbered Republicans by 47% to 26% and the District carried a D+12 PVI.

The incumbent congressman was Democrat Theodore Deutch who was elected to the former Florida 19th District in a special election in 2010. His legislative priorities included strengthening the health and financial security of retirees, helping small business and protecting national security. He faced no opposition in the Democratic primary.

His opponents in 2012 were Michael Trout and Cesar Henao, both whom ran without party affiliation. Deutch won with 77.8% of the vote vs. Michael Trout 13.3% vs. Cesar Henao 8.9%

District 22

The 22nd District runs along Florida's east coast from Palm Beach County to Broward County. Thirty percent of Palm Beach County is in the District and 17% of Broward. Voter registration in the new 22nd District saw Democrats increase from 37.5% to 40.8%, Republicans decrease from 37.4% to 32.3% and NPA increase from 21.4% to 23.9%. In 2012 it had a PVI of D+5.

When the new 22nd District emerged from reapportionment with a slight Democratic lean, the Republican incumbent in the old 22nd, Alan West, moved north seeking better accommodations and sought election in the newly formed 18th District. Lois Frankel, Democratic Mayor of West Palm Beach who had intended to take on West, quickly found herself in a contest with another experienced elected official, Adam Hasner. Hasner, the former Republican Majority Leader in the Florida House, had initially contested for the Republican nomination for US Senate and had positioned himself as the most conservative candidate in that race. When Congressman Connie Mack, III entered the Senate race in November of 2011, Republican Party heavyweights urged Hasner to run for the 22nd Congressional District seat, setting up a very competitive race.

Frankel was first elected to the Florida House of Representatives in 1986 and served 14 years in that body, becoming the first woman Democratic minority leader. She was elected Mayor of West Palm Beach in 2003 when she defeated the incumbent Democrat Joel Davis and went on to serve 8 years in that office. An aggressive, outspoken liberal in the legislature, she championed AIDS legislation and fought for healthcare and social programs. As mayor she was sometimes viewed as abrasive and reputedly would stonewall opponents. In the Congressional campaign, she defended her tenure as mayor and supported President Obama's Affordable Care Act and the president's proposal to raise taxes on those who annually make $250,000 or more.

Hasner won his first legislative seat in 2002 and became House Majority Leader in 2007. In the following year he became the first House member to raise $1 million in political contributions. (Sherman, 2012). Subsequently he became the "consummate Republican–down to his red, white and blue boots made from elephant skin," and bragged that Marco Rubio, the State's Republican US Senator once called him "the most partisan Republican in Tallahassee." (Ibid) Facing a more moderate electorate In the Congressional campaign than he had in the Republican primary for the US Senate, he backed off from the stance he had taken as an extreme conservative in that primary and retracted his initial support for GOP Representative Paul Ryan's budget plan which would convert Medicare to a voucher plan and called for repeal of Obamacare. Both Hasner and Frankel raised and spent more than $3 million (Frankel $3.4 and Hasner $3.2) in their campaigns with Frankel winning by 54.6% to 45.4% for Hasner.

District 23

The "new" District 23 was largely a restructured version of the previous District 20, eliminating "fingers" of territory that wound around to some cities while avoiding others. It included portions of Broward and Miami-Dade Counties. The new District was 25.5% Republican, 51.1% Democratic, 21.2% unaffiliated and had a very large Jewish populations. It had a D+11 PVI in 2102 and had been represented since 2004 by Debbie Wasserman Schultz, a highly visible Democrat on the national scene who was Chair of the Democratic National Committee and a Deputy Whip in the US House of Representatives.

To run against Ms Wasserman Schultz in a heavily Democratic district, the Republicans nominated for a second time their unsuccessful candidate from 2010, Karen Harrington, who had campaigned by disagreeing with Wasserman Schultz on virtually every issue and had lost by 60% to 38%. In 2012, she tried to tie Wasserman Schultz to President Obama and suffered an even worse fate than in 2010, losing by 63.2% to 35.6%. In the aftermath of the election one conservative columnist pointed out, "Lady Gaga had a better chance of becoming Pope than Harrington had of beating Wasserman Schultz." (Fumari, 2012).

District 24

In the aftermath of the 2011 reapportionment, Florida's 24th District closely resembled the "old" 17th District. It is located primarily in Miami-Dade County, with Broward County making up 18% of the population. Another "minority/majority" district, the 24th is heavily Democratic and dominated by African Americans (54.3%), some of whom are Haitians, and Hispanics (28.4%), with Caucasians making up 11.5% of the population. In 2012 it had a D+33 PVI.

The Democratic incumbent in 2012 was Frederica Wilson who represented the 17th District in 2010. Ms. Wilson had won the seat in 2010 against nine other Democratic candidates who were running in a competitive race for the first time since 1992 when the Meek family - first Carrie Meek and then her son, Kendrick Meek - dominated politics in the District. Wilson won the seat when four Haitian candidates split that vote, leaving Rudolph Moise, a wealthy MD/lawyer/businessman in second place. Convincing other Haitians to forego the race, Dr. Moise tried again in 2012.

Dr. Moise, who funded a significant portion of his own campaign, expressed respect for Ms. Wilson, but scorned "career politicians" and argued that it was time for "new leadership" to rejuvenate the struggling 24th District, one of the nation's most impoverished. In a somewhat controversial coup, he secured the endorsement of Michel Martelly, the President of Haiti.

Ms. Wilson cited her long list of accomplishments in Congress–including a $174,000 grant for a North Miami Haitian museum - and her experience there. She said "you have to know the process, the players. Congress is serious business. You can't gamble with neophytes. It's not a place to train politicians" (Gibson, 2012).

The decision was difficult for Haitians. North Miami's elected city clerk Michael Etienne said "we're stuck between a rock and a hard place. Of course the Haitian-American community would love to send a Haitian-American to Congress. But the community won't forget the contributions that Frederica Wilson has made" (Caputo, 2012).

Both candidates raised over $500,000 and campaigned actively. In the end, President Obama endorsed Ms. Wilson and she won by 66.4% of the vote to 33.6%.

District 25

Florida's 25th District is one of the largest in the state, stretching from the Western edge of Collier County to the eastern edge of Broward. In 2011 it was created from sections of old Districts, 14, 16, 17, 18, 21, 23, and 25. The new district held about 55% of the old 21st. In 2012, the District carried a PVI of R+9 and the incumbent was the Republican from the small remaining portion of the old 25th, Mario Diaz-Balart.

The race for the seat in 2012 was one-sided. The incumbent had served in the Florida legislature of 14 years and in Congress for 10. He had a reputation for being a budget hawk and for supporting minority rights. He was also the founder and co-chairman of the Everglades Caucus, which focused on the well-being of this important economic engine in the District. He also raised nearly 4 times the money as did his opponent.

Sensing doom, the Democrats nominated Sidney Blumenthal, an eighty seven year old retired radio officer from the Merchant Marines who had been a Communist in the 1960's and who had been brought before the House Un-American Activities Committee for questioning. His primary advertising strategy was to post his platform in newspaper ads. Diaz-Belart won 75.6% of the vote.

District 26

One of two new districts awarded Florida in 2012, District 26 included parts of Monroe and Miami-Dade counties and included the Southern parts of the former 21st, 25th and 18th Districts. The District is the southernmost in the State and has one of the largest Hispanic populations in the nation. In 2012, Hispanics made up 67% of the population. Registered voters are split fairly evenly between Democrats and Republicans, with 138,885 registered Republicans and 132,778 registered Democrats. In 2012, the District carried an R+4 PVI.

The general election in 2012 in the 26th District pitted two candidates against each other who had been opponents in 2010 in the old 25th District; David Rivera, the Republican incumbent and Joe Garcia, the Democrat challenger. In that election, the candidates differed largely on Cuba–a key issue in the District and particularly for older Cubans–with Rivera espousing a hard line and Garcia supporting family travel and remittances to the island.

In 2012, however, Rivera's new district was slightly less Republican than his older one and during his first term in Congress he came under three criminal investigations and was charged with violating 11 ethics laws. Despite the endorsement of Senator Marco Rubio, he was unsuccessful in his attempts to paint Garcia as corrupt and lost by 53.6% to 43%, becoming the "first Miami-Dade congressional incumbent to lose his seat in recent memory." (Mazzel and Sheridan, 2012)

District 27

District 27, the second new Congressional District awarded to Florida in 2012 was created out of portions of what had been Districts 18, 21 and 25. It encompassed various islands stretching off the state's southern coastline, but included land area in only two counties, Miami-Dade and Monroe. Like its neighboring 26th District, the 27th is heavily Hispanic and this population demographic makes up 67% of the total population. Also like the 26th District, the 27th registers voters in nearly even numbers. Republicans claim 135,885 registrants while Democrats have 132,775 supporters.

In the 2012 race in this District, the Republican incumbent was Ileana Ros-Lehtinen who in 2010 represented the old District 18. First elected in 1989, Ros-Lehtinen had been the first Hispanic woman ever elected to Congress. Conservative, but not radically so, Ros-Lehtinen has been a reliable and dignified representative of her district over the years who has some support among Florida Democratic office holders. In 2012, she easily defeated her Democratic opponent Manny Yevancey, who some speculated had been put up by the Democratic Congressional Campaign Committee to discourage a serious Democrat from running. Yevancy did not run a campaign and his only activity appeared to be filing his statement of candidacy. He filed no FEC report, which means he raised less than $5,000. While Ros-Lehtinen spent $1.2M on the campaign, Yevancy still won 36.9% of the vote compared to 60.2% for Ros-Lehtinen, suggesting the District may be amenable to a Democratic candidate in the future.

THE PATTERN OF OUTCOMES
IN THE 2012 CONGRESSIONAL ELECTIONS

In 1990 for the first time since Reconstruction, the Republicans won the majority of Congressional seats in Florida. Since that year, they increased their numbers in every election through 2004, lost modest numbers in 2006 and 2008 and increased again in 2010. In 2012, they maintained the same number of seats they had claimed in 2010, but lost the two additional seats created as a result of the increased population of Florida reflected in the 2010 Census. Thus, their margin became 19 to 8 and their percentage of the total declined, but only to 70%, still an overwhelming majority in a highly competitive state. In this section of the book we examine the patterns of outcomes in these 2012 races and compare them to previous years and to the nation as a whole.

Party Success

In the 2012 election, the Republicans maintained their dominance in the Florida Congressional delegation. In 2010, the GOP held 19 of the state's 25 congressional seats. In the aftermath of the decennial census, the state of Florida moved ahead of New York in population size, became the nation's third largest state and was awarded two additional seats in the House of Representatives. As a result, the state's congressional delegation was increased from 25 to 27. In the 2010 election, the Republicans won 19 of these 27 seats, thus maintaining their superiority in the delegation. Despite this success, the percentage of seats controlled by the Republicans decreased by 6% between 2010 and 2012, from 76% to 70%, as Democrats won 2 additional seats.

Incumbency Success

As is typically the case in elections in the United States, incumbent members of Congress in Florida were successful in regaining their seats in the 2012 elections. Fifteen of the 19 members who sought re-election achieved it, a success rate of 79%. It's good to be an incumbent if you want to hold public office. While 79% is an impressive number, it is actually the lowest Congressional incumbent success rate in Florida history and continues a decline in this rate that began in in 2006.

In part, the "low" success rate in 2012 was a product of the reapportionment of 2011, when all districts were re-drawn and some incumbents were thrown into districts against others and compelled to compete against their own "political kin" in party primaries. Two of the four losses in 2012 came about in this fashion; Republican Cliff Stearns lost to a challenger from his own party in his new district and Republican Sandy Adams lost to Republican John Mica when they were thrown against each other in the newly created 7th District. Two other Republicans, David Rivera and Allen West lost to Democrats, but especially in the West case, reapportionment played a strong role in the outcome also.

For most of the state's history, incumbents in Florida achieved greater re-election success than did those in the nation as a whole. In 2008, this pattern began to change and in 2008, 2010 and 2012, the incumbency success rate in Florida declined steadily and lagged behind that of the nation as a whole. In 2012, ninety three percent (93%) of congressional incumbents who sought re-election in the US were successful. (Abrahamson, Gomez, and Rohde. 2012).

In general, Florida is a competitive state. Democrats and Republicans register to vote in very similar numbers (4.7 million Dems to 4.2 Reps) and roughly equal percentages of citizens self-identify with the two parties (44.7%D to 40.2%R)[1] Thus close elections are to be expected and some changes are likely to occur in any given year.

Losses/Gains by the Party of the President

Congressional elections are strongly affected by those of the president. When the president is on the ballot, voter turnout increases which affects voting for candidates for Congress. Furthermore, the president's approval rating affects the level and direction of the vote for down ticket races. Thus, political analysts tie congressional electoral success and failure directly to the president by calculating the extent to which the party of the president gains or loses congressional seats.

In general, the party of the president gains seats in Congress when the president is also on the ticket, and loses them in off-year elections when the president does not run for re-election. In only 5 elections between 1932-2012 did the party of the president lose seats in Congress during a presidential election year. In all other such years, the party of the president gained Congressional seats. (Gerhard Peters2012. This pattern occurred again in 2012 when the Democratic Party, with Barack Obama on the ticket, picked up 8 seats in Congress around the nation.

Florida contributed solidly to this pattern in 2012 when the Democrats picked up two seats. In a re-run between the two candidates who had competed in 2010, Democrat Joe Garcia beat David Rivera in the 26th District and Democrat Patrick Murphy beat Allen West in District 18. Thus, in 2012, the Republicans controlled "only" 70% of the Florida congressional delegation as opposed to 76% in 2010.

Electoral Competitiveness

Throughout history, congressional elections in Florida have not been very competitive. That is, incumbents usually win, they often win by large margins and many times, they do not even draw competition from their major party opponent, drawing instead a candidate who either runs without partisan attachment (NPA) or who represents a small, not very well known party that has little chance of winning.

Over the time period, 1982–2004, nearly 80% of all congressional elections in Florida were "landslides" meaning that the margin of victory in the race was greater than 20%. For a brief four year period in 2006 and 2008, the pattern of competitiveness improved when the landslide index fell to 56%. However, in 2010 *and again in 2012*, competitiveness in the state decreased and the landslide index rose to 70%. Put differently, the average winner in a congressional race in Florida in 2012 garnered 30 per cent (30.1%) more votes than did the average next highest finisher in these races. Many political pundits suggest that campaigns are no longer competitive when the differences between winners and losers is 10% or greater. If this is correct, then the *average* Congressional race in Florida is highly non-competitive. Not so good for democracy.

IV

The State Legislative Campaigns

Chapter Ten

The State Legislative Races

INTRODUCTION

Although each election year is unique, the 2012 election for the Florida State Legislature was particularly so in that the districts in which candidates competed were different from those in which they had run in the 2010 elections. As a result of the population changes enumerated in the 2010 decennial census, the boundaries of each district were re-drawn and virtually all of the candidates in 2012 were forced to run in districts that were somewhat different from those in which they had been candidates in 2010. As a result, several incumbents retired, others were thrown into competition, both in their own party primaries or in the general election of against other incumbents. Despite these changes, or perhaps because of them, legislative reapportionment had only marginal effect on the overall outcome of the election, and a similar effect in more specific elements of legislative behavior, e.g., incumbency success, overall competitiveness and gains/losses of the party of the president. We review these outcomes in the following pages.

THE PARAMETERS OF THE 2012 LEGISLATIVE SESSION

As the 2010 election year opened, the Republican Party dominated the Florida State Legislature. The GOP has held control of the Florida State Senate since 1994 and the Florida House of Representatives since 1996, and in 2010 they held super majorities in both Houses. Seventy percent of the seats in the state senate (70%) were Republican and 67% of the members of the House of Representatives were also Republicans. The Democrats faced a bleak landscape, hoped to make modest gains in membership and to avoid the kind of debilitating setback they had suffered in the aftermath of the reapportionment of 2001. The Republicans hoped to maintain their numerical superiority in both houses and to use their control of the reapportionment process to do so.

Unsettled by the prospect of having Barack Obama at the head of the Democratic ticket and a repetition of the high Democrat turnout in 2008, in 2011 Florida Republicans passed HB 1355 which cut early voting days from 14 to eight, restricted the activities of voter registration organizations like the League of Women Voters and made it harder for voters who had changed counties since the last election to cast ballots. Critics, and even some Republicans, claimed that these provisions were designed to suppress the Democratic Party vote. (Kam and Lanigua, 2012)

Furthermore, astute observers of the 2012 elections expected the Republicans controlling the reapportionment process to ensure that their party maintained control of the legislature and most predicted that the Democrats would win small numbers of new seats. Christian Ulvert, a consultant working for the state Democratic Party said, "we didn't lose a bunch of districts overnight and we're not going to win a bunch of districts overnight." (Dunkelberger. 2012). The fact that 2012 was a presidential election year gave some hope to the Democrats as the party of the president typically picks up seats in state legislatures when their president is at the top of the ticket.

The Senate Landscape

Politics are different in reapportionment years than in normal years and the electoral context is substantially disturbed by the changes wrought in re-districting. New district lines create vacancies as well as contests between incumbents and all district boundaries are altered in some degree. In addition, ten Senators met Florida's constitutional term limits provision and were not eligible for re-election. This gave those re-drawing the districts some flexibility since there was no imperative to protect their seats.

A particularly important feature of the 2012 Senate environment was that all 40 districts in the Senate were in play simultaneously, while in non-reapportionment years only a portion of the Florida State Senate is up for re-election. Thus the number of candidates who sought these offices increased from 60 in 2010 to 91 in 2012, the total cost of the election was expected to rise and the level of competitiveness in the elections also potentially increased. Thus, political observers in Florida anticipated substantial turnover in personnel in the Senate between 2010 and 2012, but with little change in partisan control. A new Hispanic district in Central Florida was projected as a new Democrat seat, but the Florida Chamber of Commerce projected only one or two more Democratic victories. (Dunkelberger, 2012)

The House Landscape

All one hundred twenty (n=120) House seats were up for election in 2012 and because of reapportionment each had different physical boundaries than had been the case in 2010. Furthermore, term limits bumped 12 members (2 Democrats and 10 Republicans) from the list of those eligible to run in these new districts. In theory, these circumstances agued well for a competitive electoral cycle and 294 candidates ran for the positions. Nevertheless, Republican control of the reapportionment process led skeptics to question the extent to which all districts would be competitive and the analysis by the Florida Chamber of Commerce cited above suggested that Republican performance in the election could range from a gain of one seat to a loss of five. (Dunkelberger, 2012)

OVERALL RESULTS

The re-arrangement of state legislative districts in the 2012 election and the effect of the state's term limits were expected to create opportunities for new faces in the legislature and for the Democratic Party to gain seats, and these effects were seen in the results. In the State Senate, 35% (n=14) of the incumbents from 2010 did not seek re-election, 9 because of term limits and five others because of personal or political reasons. In the House of Representatives, 34 incumbents (or 28%) did not run in 2012, 10 of these as a result of term limits. Altogether, 30% of the Florida legislators who served in 2010 did not seek re-election in 2012.

These conditions, as well as the effects of the many campaigns mounted by both parties, produced a gain of two seats in the State Senate by the Democrats and 8 seats in the House of Representatives. *Nevertheless, the Republicans maintained a 65% majority in the Senate and a 61.6% margin in the House of Representatives.* While these are substantial majorities they both fall short of a super majority where the Republicans would be able to ignore Democrats entirely. Several factors accounted for this result.

First, the Republicans were the beneficiaries of substantially greater monetary resources than were the Democrats. The total of all campaign contributions made to Republican state legislative campaign organizations in 2012 was nearly three times that of the contributions made to the Democrats. Republican candidates reported $21.8 million in contributions and Democrats reported $7.4 million. The average amount raised by Republicans in the general election was $294,081, for Democrats it was $81 thousand (2012)

Second, HB1355 passed in 2010, had the effect that participants in the political process in Florida claim was the law's intent. That was to make voting more burdensome for minority voters and African Americans in particular who are a mainstay of the Democratic Party's coalition. (Herron and Smith, 2012)

Third, many journalists and other political observers claim that the Republicans benefited from the manner in which legislative districts were redrawn in the 2011 reapportionment plan. These boundaries were drawn in compliance with the Fair Districts constitutional amendment adopted by Floridians in 2010, which was designed to ensure that partisanship would be removed from the factors utilized in drawing district lines and was intended to prevent the majority party in the state legislature from utilizing its control over the reapportionment process to prejudice legislative boundaries in its favor. The new Congressional and State Senate boundaries released in 2011 were immediately challenged in state court by the League of Women Voters as violating the Fair Districts amendment, but with no time to hear the case in court, these districts served as the parameters of the 2012 election. And these parameters likely gave the Republicans the advantage. In a state where registered Democrats outnumber registered Republicans by 4.7 million to 4.2 million and where 44.7% of residents identified with the Democratic Party as opposed to 40.2% with the Republicans, the Republicans maintained massive majorities in both houses of the Florida State Legislature.

Senate Outcomes

In reapportionment years, all State Senate Seats are up for re-election and in 2012 forty new senate seats were open. The Republicans won 26 of these seats while the Democrats captured 14. The results represented a gain of two (n=2) seats by the Democrats.

Despite the opportunity created by the large number of open seats, only 29 of these seats had contests in the general election – 11 candidates ran unopposed - and in general, the Senate races in 2012 were very uncompetitive. Twenty percent of the elections had margins of victory greater than 40%, another twenty percent were separated by margins between 21 and forty percent and 27.5% were decided by margins between 5 and 10 percent. No race was decided by a margin of less than 5%.

Many political consultants feel that only political campaigns decided by margins of 10 percent or less are truly competitive and that any losing candidate in a race decided by a margin greater than that really had no chance of victory. If this standard is applied in the Florida Senate races of 2012, then *fewer than 1% of the races were truly competitive*, those in districts 24 and 34. In 2010, 10 Senate seats were decided by these margins, making 2012 a particularly uncompetitive year.

Political observers also classify campaigns decided by margins of 20% or greater as "landslides." The Florida Senate *had* 16 races (or 40% of the total) decided by these margins in 2012. Another 27.5% of the races were decided by margins of 11-20 percent. It is hard to believe that outcomes such as these came randomly from districts that were designed to give Floridians equal representation and competitive elections.

In the following paragraphs we provide a short description of the two races that had genuine competition.

Senate District 24

This district is located entirely within Hillsborough County, a mix of suburbs, small businesses and farms. It includes conservative east Hillsborough County, an area called New Tampa and neighborhoods near the University of South Florida. While voter registration figures are relatively equal – 104,530 Republican, 102,074 Democrat and 69,730 NPA - it was generally considered a relatively safe Republican district and enjoyed an aggressive primary battle in that party.

The winner of the Republican primary was Tom Lee, a home builder from Brandon who had run for the position of Florida's Chief Financial Officer in 2006 and had served in the state senate from 1996 to 2006, and was Senate President in the last two of these years. Mr. Lee wanted to "maintain low taxes and have minimal regulation requirements in order to attract new business."

Mr. Lee's opponent was Democrat Elizabeth Belcher, a first time candidate who had been a criminal investigator for the Internal Revenue Service for 27 years before retiring in 2007. Her platform included "saving taxpayers' money by stopping the bribery to the large corporations to relocate to Florida. Take that money and direct it to small businesses already here to expand and to help start new local businesses." (Ibid)

This race was described by some as a David vs Goliath contest with Lee the Goliath. The former senator was well connected in Republican politics in Florida, garnered a number of high visibility endorsements, Jeb Bush, etc., and raised $531,000 from a wide range of businesses and conservative groups. Ms. Belcher had no support from the Democratic Party and raised only $13,725. Nevertheless, she knocked on doors and talked to voters about what she wanted to do in Tallahassee and lost by only 8% of the vote. Either Goliath was not as big as was thought, Ms. Belcher was a better campaigner than was though or the district is more competitive than was thought.

Senate District 34

This district runs along the Atlantic Coast from Boynton Beach to Fort Lauderdale. Roughly equal parts of the district are in Broward and Palm Beach Counties. This new district was the only one in which two incumbents were thrown against each other in the 2010 election and it contained portions of old Senate district 25 (held by Republican Ellen Bogdanoff) and Senate district 30 (held by Democrat Maria Sachs). Much of the new district had been represented by Bogdanoff prior to the reapportionment, but Democrats in the new district had a 9 point advantage in voter registration. Nevertheless, Bogdanoff was an effective campaigner and a formidable fundraiser and most observers of Florida politics predicted a close race.

This race had particular importance for both parties since a Republican victory would give that party a super majority in the Senate, allowing them to make policy with complete disregard for Democratic views. Contrarily, a Democratic victory would salvage a sliver of influence for that party. Thus both parties made the seat their top state senate priority and pledged their help to the respective campaigns. Don Gaetz, the incoming Republican president of the state senate said he would spend "as much money as necessary" on the Bogdanoff campaign. (Haughney. 2012). Rod Smith, the Chair of the Florida Democratic Party said "whatever it takes, however long it takes, whatever the work is, we're going to do it because we're going to win this race." (Bennett, 2012)

Both candidates were experienced public officials. Bogdanoff, an attorney, served in the Florida House of Representatives from 2004 through 2008 and had been elected Majority Whip in 2006. She was elected to the state senate in 2010. Maria Sachs, also a lawyer, had been an assistant state attorney in Miami-Dade and Broward Counties before being elected to the Florida House of Representatives in 2006 and subsequently to the State Senate, in 2010. While in the legislature, Bogdanoff had focused on business, child care and gambling. As a Democrat in a top heavy Republican Senate, Sachs had been reduced to showing her colors by opposing issues supported by the Republicans, in particular the privatization of prisons and a "half baked" plan to "allow private charter school companies to take over public schools if enough parents could be persuaded to endorse the idea." (VerSteeg. 2012.)

Given the stakes in the race, control of the chamber by a super majority, both candidates campaigned furiously, expensively and negatively. Bogdanoff, a Jew, claimed that Sachs, also Jewish, had voted against Holocaust funding (Abramson. 2012) "Bogdanoff Chastised for Republican Mailer Saying Sachs Voted Against Holocaust Funding" (Palm Beach Post. 2012). and sent out mailers charging that Sachs had used a car service to take her to the airport without providing receipts for the $7,000 expenditure of state funds and hinted that she was under investigation for her finances (Haughney, 2012). The Democrat countered by claiming that Bogdanoff should be "accused of crimes of child abandonment and senior abuse and neglect because of her votes to cut education funding and cap lawsuits in wrongful death cases against nursing homes" (Ibid).

In the end the efforts of the Sachs campaign combined with President Obama's presence on the ballot and his OFA organization's field work to drive up voting turnout for the Democrats and Sachs pulled out a surprising 5.6% victory. She claimed 122,430 votes to 109,329 for Bogdanoff.

House Outcomes

All 120 seats in the Florida House of Representatives were available in 2012. The Republicans captured 74 of these seats with the Democrats winning 46. These numbers represented a gain of 8 seats by the Democrats.

As was the case in the state senate, many Florida House races also went uncontested or were decided by very large margins. Forty eight percent (48.3%) of the winning candidates essentially had no opposition in their campaigns; i.e. either no other names appeared on the general election ballot with them or the opposition came from small third parties or through write in ballots. Thus, nearly one half of all Floridians (58 districts) were represented in the Florida House of Representatives by individuals who had not been required to actively articulate to the public the reasons they should be chosen to be representatives.

In addition to the 58 candidates who ran essentially unopposed, another twenty candidates won by margins between 21 and 40% and an additional eight were involved in races where the margin of victory was over 40%. Using *Fair Votes'* definition of a landslide victory (any margin over 20%), seventy one percent (71.6%) of the races for the Florida State House of Representatives in 2012 can be placed in this category. *Only 11 races (10%) were highly competitive, i.e., had margins of victory of 5% or less and only 25 (20.8%) were decided by margins of 10% or less, the traditional break-point between competitive and non-competitive races.* The latter number does represents an increase over that in 2010, when only 10% fell into this category. Nevertheless, when 80% of the elections in the state are not competitive, democracy suffers and candidate accountability is limited. (Robert Dahl, 1956).

Following are brief descriptions of the House races in which genuine competition – margins of less than 5% - took place.

House District 24

This district is composed of parts of Flagler, Volusia and St. John's counties. While Democratic leaning Flagler County made up the largest segment of the district when measured by voting age population, voter registration in the three counties was skewed slightly to the Republicans with 40.2% Republican, 33.6% Democrat and 22.9% NPA.

The Republicans chose as their candidate Travis Hutson the wealthy young scion of a local family that owned a private real estate investment business and who had never been a candidate for public office. The Democrats chose Milissa Holland, an energetic young mother who had served with great energy for six years on the Flagler County Commission and whose father had been one of the founders of Palm Coast, her home town, and who had also been a city council member. Holland made her experience as a public servant the centerpiece of her campaign, while Hutson claimed that he too had experience, "with non-profits, …with people. I understand that stuff, and I can do that stuff, so there's no difference there" (Holland, 2012).

While both candidates stressed their interest in public education, issue differences were not the focal point of the race. Instead, this campaign was essentially a contest between a candidate with high name recognition and high energy but little money and one who had lower visibility but lots of money. The Republican Party and its reservoir of special interest groups, including the Koch Brothers, generated nearly seven times the money for Hutson as did the Democrats for Holland. The fundraising totals were $285,561 for Hutson and $42,098 for Holland. (Follow the Money) Even with President Obama at the head of the ticket, Democratic voter turnout in Flagler County dropped by 10% between 2008 and 2012, Obama lost the County to Mitt Romney and Hutson pulled out a narrow victory, gaining 1,836 more votes than did Holland.

House District 29

House district 29 is located entirely within Seminole County, a strongly Republican county that has rarely elected Democrats to Congress or to the Florida State Legislature. In the aftermath of the 2012 reapportionment, the district included 42,944 Republicans registrants and 34,136 Democrats and the boundaries had been influenced by the Republican candidate in the race, Chris Dorworth, who was the incoming Speaker of the Florida House. As a key player in the reapportionment process, Dorworth had helped draw the seemingly safe seat he was running for in 2012. The Democrats chose as their candidate Mike Clelland, an attorney and a retired firefighter from Longworth, Florida.

Chris Dorworth had represented District 34 in the Florida House from 2007 through 2012 and was one of the most powerful members of the Florida Legislature. Nevertheless, "his business problems pushed his net worth into negative numbers and his home into foreclosure" critics repeatedly accused him of conflicts of interest (Garci, 2012). "Dorworth, In Line to Be House Speaker, Now in Danger of Losing His Seat Altogether." and he and the local media engaged in an on-going feud that left him with high negative ID (Torres, 2014). In spite of these problems, Dorworth raised $544,000 through his own campaign account and another $344,000 through a political committee that accepted five-figure checks from the Florida Realtors and Walt Disney World, assumed he would win and encouraged the Democrats to put money into his opponent's campaign so as to reduce their ability to help other candidates with a better chance of winning. (Garcia, 2012)

While Mike Clelland was a political novice, he made raising ethical standards in the Capitol the focal point of his campaign, "studied the issues and walked his district every day convincing voters to give him a chance." (Ravich, 2012. Until the last weeks of the campaign almost all of the money he raised in the campaign ($64,265) came from his fellow firefighters and individual citizens who believed in him. At that point a Florida Democratic Party poll showed he had a chance at victory and the Party spent $44,518 (Follow the Money 2012) on direct mail criticizing Dorworth for his home foreclosure and for allegedly living with a lover while in the midst of a bitter divorce with his ex-wife. (Garcia, 2012).

As the election returns came in on November 6, Dorworth and his Republican Party colleagues began to realize that a huge political upset was in the offing. By early Wednesday morning, Clelland led by 37 votes and after the re-count ending on the following Monday, he had enlarged this margin to 146 votes and was declared the winner. In a district where a road is named in honor of former Republican President Ronald Reagan, this represented a major shock to Republican Party fortunes.

House District 41

House District 41 is located entirely within Polk County, which in 2012 was a predominantly Democratic County, but one that routinely elects Republican candidates. In 2012, there were more registered Democrats in the 41st District than Republicans (37,703 to 33,073), but the incumbent state representative was Republican John Wood, who had to fight through a primary in order to retain his candidacy.

John Wood was the CEO of John Wood Enterprises, Agriculture and Housing Co., a lawyer and a real estate agent. His opponent in the race was Karen Cooper Welzel, a retired human resources professional who was the past chair of the Polk County Democratic Executive Committee and who was making her first attempt at elective office.

The race became a "referendum on the Republican's last two years in Tallahassee" (Ledger, 2012). Wood defended his support of Governor Rick Scott and his policies which Wood said made Florida one of the best places in the nation for business. Karen Welzel countered by arguing that Wood had no record to stand on with everyday folks. "He may be with the chamber and the real estate groups – but with everyday folks, they don't know who he is." (Ibid)

As an incumbent, Wood had access to a much greater base of monetary support and succeeded in raising more than ten times the money as did Welzel, $237,191 to $17,738. This difference was undoubtedly the key factor in the campaign, as Wood won by only 2.8% of the vote (51.4% to 48.6%). In the aftermath of the campaign, an independent Democratic organization, the Political Hurricane, criticized the Florida Democratic Party for its failure to support Welzel and other similar candidates (2012). On the other hand the Republican Party put up more money for Wood, $33,200, than Welzel was able to raise in total. (Follow the Money, 2012)

House District 42

This district is located in Osceola and in Polk Counties and in 2012 showed a small Democratic lean, but one in which Republican gubernatorial candidate Rick Scott beat Democrat Alex Sink in 2010. There were 32,818 Republicans registered in the District and 37,707 Democrats. The initial Republican candidate in the district was popular and well connected incumbent Mike Horner from Kissimmee, who appeared to be cruising for re-election before his name appeared on a client list of an East Orange prostitute, after which he resigned the seat. The Democrat in the race was Eileen Game, a novice candidate whose connections with the District were minimal. She worked first for Ernst and Young as an account manager and subsequently ran a small business in Ft. Lauderdale. She lived in Avon Park and was a registered voter in Highlands County when she announced her candidacy, but moved into an apartment in Frostproof shortly thereafter. The Democratic Party of Florida gave her little chance in the race and prepared to spend its money elsewhere.

The Horner scandal changed the race dramatically. The Republicans quickly replaced Horner with Mike LaRossa, a realtor from Celebration, Florida, but unfortunately for LaRossa, Mike Horner's name remained on the ballot and forced LaRossa into a campaign where he had to raise his own name recognition and to inform voters that a vote for Horner was a vote for LaRossa. While Game's chances improved dramatically, her inexperience was evident and some complained that she still campaigned as if she had little chance in the race. In addition, the Democratic Party seemed hesitant about backing her strongly and committed only $31,000 to her campaign.

The Republicans, hoping to save an incumbent seat, rallied strongly and the Chairman of the Osceola County Party led the effort to inform voters of the ballot issue with a strong recorded telephone campaign and a media blitz, and the Republican Party of Florida put $100,000 into LaRossa's race.

The two candidates campaigned on traditional party platforms. LaRossa wanted less taxes and regulations so that small businesses may grow and create jobs, while Game favored more emphasis on education in order to help people secure good paying jobs.

The inexperience of the Democratic candidate and the strong support provided LaRossa by his party (the Republican had a three to one advantage in fundraising over his Democratic opponent: $167,382 to $55,774) enabled him to eke out a 2.5% victory and save an incumbent seat.

District 47

District 47 is located entirely within Orange County and is slightly Republican, with 42,829 registered voters for that party compared with 41,095 Democrats and 25,782 NPA. In 2010, the seat was held by Republican James Grant who was moved to District 64 in reapportionment leaving #47 open. Both the Democrats and the Republicans nominated candidates without opposition in their primaries and set out to capture the seat.

The Democratic candidate was Linda Stewart, a resident of Orlando who had served two terms on the Orange County Commission. The Republicans chose Bob Brooks, an MD who had served two terms in the Florida House in the mid- 1990's. The candidates epitomized core values in their parties and the race "mirrored other contests with business groups such as the Florida Chamber of Commerce backing the Republican Brooks, and unions and the Sierra Club behind Stewart. "

The Brooks campaign raised more than two and one half times the amount of money as did Stewart ($410,519 to $159,440) and blasted her for past support for potential gas-or sales-tax hikes for transit, dubbing her "bad medicine for jobs." (Ibid) Stewart attacked Brooks for his support of charter schools and "school voucher schemes that drains millions of our tax dollars from public schools." (Ibid) The two candidates also differed on requiring a 24 hour waiting period before an abortion and requiring on-line retailers to pay state sales tax.

Stewart's more-recent service as County commissioner arguably gave her higher name recognition and the strong effort made by the Obama campaign increased Democratic voter turnout. The *Orlando Sentinel* endorsed Stewart for distinguishing herself on growth management issues and diversifying the region's economy and she slipped by Brooks by 52% to 48% of the vote.

District 59

This District is located entirely within Hillsborough County and leans slightly Democratic, with 37,622 such voters as compared to 34,741 Republicans. Before the 2010 reapportionment, the incumbent legislator was Democrat Betty Reed who was shifted into District 61 for the 2012 race.

In 2012, the Republicans nominated Russ Spano a lawyer from Riverview, Fl. who practiced there in his own small firm. His opponent, Gail Gottleib was born and raised in Brandon and was also an attorney. She had served in the Peace Corps and worked in several humanitarian organizations in Washington, DC.

This was another race in which the candidates attempted to tie their opponents to what they believed were the weak points of their respective political parties. Thus Gottleib focused on Republican Party efforts to provide tax breaks to corporations who shifted their profits to out-of-state subsidiaries and to incorporate offshore. She also attacked Republican cuts in education.

Spano, on the other hand, tried to tie Gottlieb to what he claimed were the radical ideas of the Democratic Party. A campaign direct mailer showed images of bomb-throwing terrorists and threatening demonstrators, and claimed that "Gail Gottleib is trying to bring her brand of radical chaos to Eastern Hillsborough County." They claimed she was "too liberal, too Washington, D.C., too extreme."

Once again, the Republican candidate nearly trebled the amount of money raised by the Democrats. Spano collected $265,455 and Gottlieb took in $80,533. The RPF contributed $72,726 to its candidate while only the Hillsborough County Democratic Party contributed to Gottlieb's account ($4,000). With the presidential campaign a virtual tie and providing no advantage to either party, Spano won by a narrow 50.7% to 49.3%, a 1,051 vote margin.

District 63

Another district located entirely within Hillsborough County, District 63 included the communities of Lutz, New Tampa, Town 'N Country, Egypt and Ybor City. In the aftermath of the 2010 reapportionment, the District was left leaning Democrat, with 38,176 in that Party, 32,211 Republicans and 24,517 NPA.

The Republican candidate in the race was Shawn Harrison, an attorney who represented nursing homes, and who had represented District 60 in the 2010 election. The Democrats chose Mark Danish, a seventh grade science teacher in New Tampa. As reported by the *Tampa Bay Times*, the two candidates differed substantially in their political views.

Danish, a member of the state's teacher's union, focused on support for public education, on improving the state's infrastructure, on making long-term investments in clean energy and on eliminating loopholes in the state's "unfair" tax system.

Harrison wanted to offer tax incentives that attract business to Florida and to "foster an environment where business feels confident coming to Florida, perhaps by working with local governments to offer incentives." He also though that Florida "doesn't have an income problem, it has a spending problem."

Making a strong effort to protect one of its incumbents, the Republican Party of Florida put $166,554 into Harrison's campaign fund and other interests tied to the Republican Party boosted the campaign total to $465,554.

(Follow the Money, 2012) Mark Danish was left on his own by the Florida Democrats and was able to raise only $19,560.

Relying on his friends and family, including his son Michael, the Danish campaign "mapped out a road to victory. We came in with a really tight strategy on how we wanted to target the district. Whoever won New Tampa would pretty much win the District." (Middle School Teacher Ousts Incumbent in Race for House Seat in District 63. (Miesel 2014). Relying on volunteers, the Danish campaign walked "every inch of the surrounding neighborhood." (Ibid) His campaign was boosted by the presence of Barack Obama on the presidential ticket and voter turnout in New Tampa, usually lower than the rest of Hillsborough County, exceeded that of the County as a whole by nearly 6%. Danish won Tampa City by 49% to 44% as compared to 50.5% to 49.4% county-wide. These results pushed Danish ahead by only 728 votes. This result was one of the biggest upsets in Florida in the 2012 election year.

District 69

District 69 lies entirely within Pinellas County, a county that overall is slightly Democratic in registration, but which leaned slightly Republican, with 41,665 voters compared to 40,778 Democrats. The incumbent in the seat in 2010 was Republican Ray Pilon who was moved to District 72, producing an open seat in 69.

After a spirited primary, the Republicans nominated Kathleen Peters, a mother of four who had served as Mayor of South Pasadena and on the city council of that city. She had also worked for the Clearwater Chamber of Commerce. The Republican Party of Florida quickly rushed in to support her with a contribution of $122,146 and contributors aligned with that Party raised her total to $261,463 (Follow the Money, 2010)

Unwilling to place herself on the continuum of conservatism, (Politico, 2014). Ms. Peters ran on a moderate Republican platform of support for education as a way to improve the state's economy. She said "I believe our greatest investment for economic growth will be made through an investment in human capitol." (Ibid) She also supported a comprehensive energy policy designed to reduce demand versus consuming more.

The Democratic candidate was Josh Shulman, a St. Petersburg financial planner who had recently lost a bid for that town's City Council. He based his campaign on the need for change in Tallahassee, saying the Republican-led legislature had failed to address the needs of middle class Floridians like himself and his neighbors. He also blasted Peters for raising Pinellas taxes four years in a row while on the city council in South Pasadena.

While the Democratic Party supported Shulman, the always cash-starved Party was able to contribute only a fraction ($38,793) of what the Republicans contributed to Peters, and Shulman's total fundraising, $111,719, was less than half of Peters' total. (Follow the Money, 2010)

Despite a 26,000 vote victory for President Obama in Pinellas County, Ms. Peters was able to capitalize on her experience in public office and her sizeable monetary advantage to win HD 69 by a narrow 4.6% of the vote. She received 40,164 votes to 36,577 for Shulman.

District 84

This District is composed of parts of the City of Port St. Lucie, the City of Fort Pierce and the related beaches in St. Lucie County. A strong Democratic county, it had been represented in 2010 by a Democrat, Mack Bernard, who chose not to run for re-election. The resignation prompted a spirited Democratic primary that was won by insurance agent Larry Lee, Jr., a first time candidate for public office. Michelle Miller, also from Port St. Lucie, was chosen as the Republican candidate. Ms. Miller, also an insurance agent, was a veteran of the US Army who had a broad community service background.

In an unusual race, both candidates emphasized the need to run positive campaigns and to work for the benefit of all citizens of the district. Lee campaigned on his history of working with people of both parties and said "I think my opponent is a wonderful person, and that's all I'd like to say about her, emphasizing the fact that the two were friends." (Miller responded in kind, saying "I don't approve of attacking another person's character in an election." (Meisel. 2012). Unfortunately for her, the Republican Party of Florida did not agree and ran a series of negative ads against Lee that Lee said helped him win the election. Peters said "my campaign has been 100 percent positive," that all of her campaign money was spent on ads stressing reasons why people should voter for her and that she was not responsible for the GOP-funded ads that claimed Lee had paid his taxes late. "I wish the ads had been positive", she said. (Ibid)

The District was tough for any Republican. The Democrats had a 12,000 person registered voter advantage over the Republicans, President Obama won the county by 9,000 votes and Lee raised $220,881 to $147,507 for Miller; $91,545 of that coming from the Republican Party of Florida. Nevertheless, the vote was close and Miller lost by only 4.2% of the vote.

District 114

This district lies wholly within Miami-Dade County and is the most "Miami" section of the County; one that has a relatively high percentage of Hispanic voters and a slightly higher percentage of the vote that is registered Republican, in this case 37.7% to 34.8%. The race in 2012 featured Republican Erik Fresen who had held the house seat in District 111 in 2010 before reapportionment and Democrat Ross Hancock, a self-recruited first time candidate.

Fresen had been first elected in 2008 and had become a reliable conservative Republican who supported tax incentives to generate economic activity, charter schools as an alternative to the existing public school system and casinos. He served on the House Education and Finance and Tax Committees.

Ross Hancock, a former newspaper editor and a communications executive for the non-profit American Welding Society ran unopposed in the Democratic primary and generated very little support from the Florida Democratic Party. His platform focused on environmental protection, protecting the coastline and Everglades restoration. He was also a strong opponent of casinos (Politico, 2014).

As an incumbent, Fresen had access to multiple sources of campaign finance and raised $212,795 on his own and the Republican Party of Florida added $73,456 to that total, giving him a budget of $286,251. Hancock, on the other hand, raised only $11,356, including $6,900 of his own money. The financial disparity was too much for Hancock to overcome. Nevertheless, Fresen won by only 2.2% of the vote, 30,842 to 29,439.

District 120

This District includes all of Monroe County, the Florida Keys, and part of Miami-Dade. A slightly leaning Democratic County (voter registration: 34.8% to 27.7%), the incumbent Democrat legislator was House Minority Leader Ron Sanders who termed out in 2012, leaving an open seat. Reflecting the competitive nature of the district, his predecessor had been a Republican and the Republican Gubernatorial candidate had won the district in 2010.

The Republicans nominated Holly Raschein, a former lobbyist and legislative staffer who had worked for both of the previous two representatives, one Republican and one Democrat. While she described herself as a social moderate and fiscal conservative, the focal point of her campaign was opposition to President Obama's landmark health care legislation designed to provide affordable health care to low income Americans. Backed heavily by the RPOF ($113,076) and tied to that Party's long list of supporters, she raised a total of $359,076 for her campaign.

The Democrats nominated Ian Whitney, the president of the Key West Innkeepers Association who decided to run for the position because "the legislature and the governor are taking our state in the wrong direction on issue after issue." (DeSantis, 2012)

The campaign was civil, but the candidates disagreed on most issues. Saying she was "all for health care." Raschein opposed expansion of Meidicaid to needy people even though "the district has the highest uninsured rate in the entire state," (Ibid) Whitney supported it. Raschein also supported the use of publicly supported vouchers for use by private school students, a policy that Whitney also opposed. In the end, the Raschein monetary advantage (about 3 to 1) enabled her to slip by Whitney by 4.8% of the vote.

PATTERNS IN THE OUTCOMES
OF THE FLORIDA LEGISLATIVE RACES

The individual outcomes described in the foregoing paragraphs can be aggregated into several patterns and compared to similar outcomes around the nation, thus putting legislative elections in Florida in a broader perspective. We turn now to an examination of two broader patterns.

Gains/Losses by the Party of the President

The outcomes of so-called "down ticket" races are heavily influenced by citizen attitudes about the performance of the President and of his political party and these attitudes vary from election to election. Thus, in years when candidates for congress and state legislative seats share the ticket with an incumbent president, the incumbent's party is likely to win additional seats. In contrast, in "off year" elections, the party of the president is likely to lose "down ticket" elections. These patterns are evident over the time period 1900 through the present and have also showed up in Florida. (Campbell, 1986; Crew 2013)

In Florida in 2012, the party of the president, the Democrats, picked up 10 seats in the Florida Legislature, 2 in the State Senate and 8 in the Florida House of Representatives. This result was consistent with those from the nation as a whole where the Democrats "took back about 150 seats." (National Conference of State Legislatures) Thus, the decades long trend of the party of the president gaining state legislative seats in years in which the president is on the electoral ticket continues in both the nation and in Florida.

Incumbency Success

Incumbent candidates for the Florida legislature almost always win re-election. In the ten years between 2000 and 2008, 98% of incumbents who sought re-election to the Florida legislature were successful in their quest. In 2010, this rate fell to 94.6% and in 2012 it rebounded to 95.6% when only four of 91 incumbents (one in a primary) failed in their bids for re-election. Throughout the nation in 2012, 4,534 state legislators ran for re-election around the nations. Of these only 294 failed to hold their seat, a 94% incumbency success rate (Ballotpedia, 2012). Thus, legislative races in Florida are less competitive than those in the nation as a whole.

Party Success

In 2012, for the ninth consecutive electoral cycle, control of the Florida House of Representatives remained in the hands of the Republican Party. While the size of the majority was diminished from a supermajority of 67.5% to 61.6%, the Republican Party of Florida is still dominant. The election of a Democratic presidential candidate in the state did not contribute to change in party control of the Florida legislature, a phenomenon that usually occurs in presidential year elections and which occurred in 8 states throughout the nation in 2012 (Ballotpedia, 2012).

V

What's Next in Politics in Florida?

Chapter Eleven

Patterns, Trends, and the Future of Florida Politics

INTRODUCTION

This book is the third in a series designed to place the elections in Florida in historical context. The results permit us to begin a description of long running patterns and trends in both the state's electoral system and in electoral-related features of that system. These outcomes also permit us to anticipate future electorally related prospects in the State.

TRENDS IN THE FLORIDA ELECTORAL SYSTEM

Electoral systems are comprised of the laws regarding such things as election timing, methods of nomination, formulas for deciding election outcomes, voter eligibility and the mechanics of registering and casting a ballot. These laws are not neutral; they affect electoral outcomes in a variety of ways and have been the focus of attention by political partisans over the course of both Florida and American history. Both parties have attempted to use them to their advantage.

In the aftermath of the 2000 election in Florida which saw an embarrassing array of long lines, inadequate voting facilities, problems with punch card ballots and their chads, butterfly ballots and angry voters, the state legislature began to make changes to the state's electoral system in an effort to ensure its integrity. Many of the actions necessary to improvement had bipartisan support and were relatively easy to adopt. In reforms enacted in the years 2001 to 2004, many of these deficiencies were addressed. These included standardization and uniformity of voting machines, rules for recounting ballots, and rules for counting overseas absentee ballots. They also addressed issues related to problems in registration and voting for disabled citizens and the logic and accuracy testing of voting equipment.

Subsequent issues including laws regarding voter registration processes, early voting, proof of citizenship and the voting rights of felons generated greater controversy and became enmeshed in partisan disagreement. In the following paragraphs we speak to these issues and to their effect (For an extensive analysis of this effort see Susan MacManus, 2013).

Voter Registration Rules, Early Voting and Proof of Citizenship

In May, 2011 the Florida State Legislature enacted a sweeping rewrite of the state's election laws that required provisional ballots from citizens attempting to change their name or address at the poll, cut the time for early voting from 14 days to eight, eliminated early voting on the Sunday immediately preceding Election Day, reduced the number of early voting sites available, invalidated absentee ballots if the voter's signature on the certificate did not match the signature on record at the supervisor of election's office, and required anyone signing up new voters to hand in registration forms to the state board of elections within 48 hours of collection or face felony charges and fines. It also required a specific type of picture identification in order to vote and a signature that matched exactly that in the voter registration records.

The law generated immediate partisan reaction. One observer claimed that "Republicans are doing their part ...to undermine efforts to replicate the 2008-sized turnout that put our state in the Democratic win column." (Lyons, 2011). Republicans meanwhile argued that the law was intended to protect the electoral system against fraud. GOP State Senator Michael Bennett said, "I want the people in the State of Florida to want to vote as bad as that person in Africa who is willing to walk 200 miles for that opportunity he's never had before in his life. This should not be easy." (Benton, 2012). "The League of Women Voters—an organization with a 91 year history of registering and educating voters—ceased registration efforts in the state. Subsequent research on the effect of these changes showed that Florida voters waited longer on average to cast a ballot than voters in any other state, that voter registration in late 2011 dropped precipitously compared to registration in 2007 and that Democratic, African American and Hispanic, younger and first time voters were disproportionately affected (Famighetti, Melillo, and Perez, 2012).

Felony Voting Rules

An analysis published by The Brennan Center for Justice in March, 2014, estimated that "1.5 million Florida citizens, or 10.4% of the state's voting-age population were disenfranchised because of a criminal conviction" (Brennan Center for Justice, 2014) and Florida goes beyond almost all states in efforts to restrict access to the ballot by individuals convicted of crime. The implications of this strategy go beyond questions related to theories of democracy and who is eligible to vote because the restriction has partisan implications. As well-known conservative newspaper columnist George Will points out "it is indelicate to say but indisputably true: most felons—not all; not those, for example, from Enron's executive suites—are Democrats." (Will, 2005). One analyst claims that had ex-felons voted in Florida in 2000, Al Gore would have won the election (Greenbaum, 2014).

In contrast to many states that allow felons to regain their civil rights upon completion of their sentences, Florida requires these individuals to appeal to the state's Clemency Board for restoration, a long and tortuous process. Conceding that the process involved in these appeals was restrictive and cumbersome (there is and has been a backlog of pending cases), in 2007 Governor Charlie Crist, a Republican, began to allow the automatic restoration of voting rights for felons convicted of non-violent crimes who had completed their terms. In 2011 a new policy was adopted when new Governor Rick Scott, also a Republican, issued an executive order requiring that all ex-felons wait between five and seven years before being allowed to apply to regain voting rights. The League of Women Voters, the Voting Rights Coalition and the American Civil Liberties Union said the policy is "undermining democracy," (Reid, 2014.) Despite protestations that the law discriminates against young, poorly educated citizens and minorities who are likely to vote for Democrats, the law remains in place. Without question the law limits the size of the eligible voter pool in the state.

"The trajectory of voting rights and electoral access in the US is rightly seen as a story of the progressive extension of the franchise. However, often obscured by such broad narratives is the reality that electoral reforms have worked to both expand *and* restrict the franchise for particular categories of voters." (Keith Bentele and Erin E. O'Brien, 2013) It is fair to say that since 2011, Florida's electoral system has leaned in the second direction.

TRENDS IN VOTER REGISTRATION AND VOTER TURNOUT

Voter participation in Florida has long lagged behind that in most other states and both political parties have struggled to motivate their supporters to register and to turn out on Election Day. Thus even in the highly competitive presidential race in 2012, with both parties exerting great effort to get their supporters to the polls, Florida still ranked below the midpoint among the states in turnout.

Over time, more progress has been made in voter turnout than in voter registration. For example in 1988 the state ranked 30th in the nation in the percentage of the voting age population that was *registered* but in 2014 the rank had dropped to 39[th.] However, between 2000 and 2014, voter turnout, measured as the percentage of the voting age population that *cast a ballot* increased from 47.9% to 55.1%. (United States Election Project, 2012). This increase was likely spurred by the highly competitive presidential elections in the state over this time period.

Changes in voter registration have varied across specific populations in the State and these variations have substantial political implications. Over the time period 1994 to 2014 Democrats have been in the majority in the state, but Republicans and nonpartisan voters have increased their registration numbers more than have Democrats. Further, since the 2012 presidential election in Florida, Independent and NPA registration has outpaced both Democratic and Republican registration. Democratic registration decreased by 197,108 between the two elections and Republican registration decreased by 124,743 while Independent/NPA registration increased by 44,550. Concurrently, African American and Hispanic voters, who are more likely to support Democrats than Republicans, increased at faster rates than did white voters, who are likely to support Republicans. Between 2000 and 2014, Hispanic registration increased 67 percent. Thus Florida's registered voter electorate is a good deal more diverse than it has been in the past.

Changes such as these have substantial political implications. Dustin Cable at the University of Virginia suggests that these trends are the precursor to "a fundamental realignment" that threatens Republican viability in some areas (Olorunnip, 2014).

POLITICALLY RELEVANT POPULATION TRENDS

A number of population trends in Florida have implications for the state's political future. The most important of these is the states' increased racial and ethnic diversity and in 2011, people other than whites made up 43.6% of the state's population. While African Americans have traditionally been the largest non-white segment of Florida's population and have been overwhelmingly Democrats, the increase in the number of Hispanic residents touched upon in the foregoing section is particularly relevant. In 2013, Hispanics in Florida constituted 23.6% of the total population and 17.1% of eligible voters. (Pew Research Center tabulations of 2011 ACS data) A diverse group including Puerto Ricans, Mexicans, residents of Central America and Cuba, it is predominantly Democratic in partisanship, including recently the Cubans who had long been the backbone of the Republican Party. If the population trends in Florida that were evident in the period 2010 to 2020 continue, Florida can expect to become a minority/majority state in the 2020 to 2030 decade. (Think Progress, 2012). Given the current political inclinations of these segments of the population, these trends threaten the Republican Party. The former Chairman of the Republican Party in Florida, Al Cardenas, has said that "we either accept becoming a minority party due to demographic shifts or we change our rules of engagement." (Olorunnip, 2012).

Another group, millennial voters—the age group between 18 and 36—is rapidly emerging as the dominant segment of the state's population, supplanting the age group 65 and older and beginning to rival the baby boomers (ages 50 to 68) for supremacy among age cohorts. In Florida in 2010, this group included over 4 million individuals, about 30% of the state's total. The group is politically important not only for its size, but also for its diversity and its political inclinations.

Millennials are the most racially diverse generation in American history and stand out for liberal views on many political and social issues, including a belief in an activist government and for support for same-sex marriage and marijuana legalization. They are the only generation in which liberals are not significantly outnumbered by conservatives. (Pew Research, 2014) They are also politically independent, with about half (47%) choosing not to identify with either political party, 27% identifying with Democrats and 17% as Republican. However, of the self-identified Independents, 44% leaned Democratic and 31% leaned Republican. Thus, as a group they view the Democrats more favorably than the Republicans and in the presidential elections of 2008 and 2012 were far more supportive of President Obama than were older generations. As this generation gradually replaces other age cohorts in Florida, its political philosophies and tendencies will have great weight in determining who gets elected and what public issues will be addressed, and political parties will need to accommodate their interests.

TRENDS IN CAMPAIGN FINANCE

Money has always been critical to the success of political campaigns and, like all other costs, the amount of money required to conduct these campaigns in Florida has grown substantially in recent years. Further, Florida's size, its competitiveness and its political importance make it a prized target for both political parties. Consequently, the amounts contributed, collected and employed in elections in the state, and in the US, have also grown substantially. This phenomenon has been aided by the 2009/2010 US Supreme Court decisions in *Citizens United v Federal Elections Commission* and the subsequent *McCutcheon v Federal Elections Commission.* The first of these cases struck down limits on independent campaign spending by corporations and unions and the second eliminated caps on the amount any individual can contribute to a campaign. One effect of these decisions is that "outside money" is flowing into campaigns in Florida.

THE SOURCE OF CAMPAIGN FUNDING

In the aftermath of the US Supreme Court's rulings in *Citizens United* and *McCutcheon,* multiple millions, even billions, of dollars have been channeled from a variety groups outside of candidate and political party organizations into political campaigns throughout the United States. More than $200 million of this "outside money" has poured into elections in Florida over this time period (Leary, 2014).

The impact of this volume of money has been substantial. One group of scholars has argued that the activity of the groups involved has "changed the organizational structure of American politics. The changes involve not only a deepening of networked relationships horizontally, within jurisdictions, but a new, multi-jurisdictional form of vertical networking in which national actors are deeply engaged in state elections." (Hamm; Malbin, Kettler, and Glaven, 2014). A paper presented at the 2012 meeting of the American Political Science Association, New Orleans, La. August 30-September 2) In addition, since a larger share of the funds comes from conservatives (Leary 2014) it has tilted the already conservative advantage in Florida even further in that direction. Also, since much of the money goes to "attack" ads on television and in direct mail, it increases negativity in political campaigns in the state. The money also weakens the control candidates have over their own campaign messages since it is employed to further the goals of the relevant organization which may not coincide precisely with those of individual candidates. And finally, it threatens democracy because of the ability of individuals and groups to hide their connections to the donations by funneling them through specific types of legal organizations. We see no diminution in this trend or of their effects in the future of Florida politics.

Work Cited

Abramson, Paul R., John H. Aldrich, and David W. Rohde. *Change and Continuity in the 2008 and 2010 Elections*. SAGE, 2011.

Adkins, Randall E., and Andrew J. Dowdle. "Is the exhibition season becoming more important to forecasting presidential nominations?," *American Politics Research* 29, no. 3 (2001): 283–288.

Altman, Alex. "Outstumped and Outspent, Newt Gingrich Flounders in Florida" *Time*. http://swampland.time.com/2012/01/30/out-stumped-and-out-spent-newt-gingrich-flounders-in-florida/. January 30, 2012.

Ballotpedia. 2012. "State Legislative Results." http://ballotpedia.org/State_legislative_elec tions_results,_2012#tab=Election_analysis. Accessed June 4 2015.

Crew Jr, Robert E. *"The 2008 Election in Florida: Change! But Only at the Top of the Ticket*," University Press of America, 2011.

Falcone, Michael. ABC News. "Inside Mitt Romney's Florida War Room Aides See Six Months of Preparation Paying Off." Abcnews.go.com/boogs/politics/2012/01/inside-mitt-romneys-florida. January 12, 2012.

Friedman, Emily. "A Look At Mitt Romney's Ground Game." http://abcnews.go.com/ blogs/politics/2012/01/a-look-at-mitt-romneys-florida-ground-game/. January 22, 2012.

Hayes, Stephen F. "The New Romney Firewall," *The Weekly Standard*. January 30, 2012.

Hohmann, James. "Paul Ignores Fla. At Debate, On Trail at Republican Debate." http://www.politico.com/news/stories/0112/72065_Page2.html. January 31, 2012.

Holan, Angie. "Fact-checking the US Chamber of Commerce Ad on Bill Nelson." http://www.politifact.com/florida/article/2012/may/15/fact-checking-us-chamber-commerce-ad-bill-nelson/. May 15, 2012.

Isenstadt, Alex. "How Allen West Blew It," "http://www.politico.com/news/stories/1112/84108.html. November 20, 2012.

Jackovics, Ted. "Santorum Holds On To Florida Despite Fading Organization, Visibility." www2.tbo.com/news/politics/2012/jan/30/santorum-holds- On-to- Florida-despite-fading-organi-ar-352753. Accessed January 12, 2012.

Jones, Jeffrey. "Romney Expands National GOP Lead." http://www.gallup.com/poll/ 153854/romney-challenge-midwestern-young-highly-religious-gop.aspx. April 12, 2012.

Kennedy, John. "Presidential Race Turnout Could Make the Difference in Mack-Nelson Race." *Palm Beach Post*. Nov 2, 2012.

Liebovich, Mark. "Playing Hardball Runs in the Family." www.nytimes.com/2012/10/28/us/politics/connie-mack-iv-take. October 29, 2012.

Linkins, Jack. "Bill Nelson Faces Off Against Connie Mack in Florida Senate Race." http://www.huffingtonpost.com/politics/. November 6, 2012.

Matthews, Mark. "Nelson Works Hard to Be Seen as Moderate." *Orland Sentinel*, October 26, 2012.

Manjarres, Javier. "Brett Doster to Head Connie Mack's Grassroots Efforts." http://shark-tank-com/2012/05/06brett-doster-to-head-connie-macks. May 6, 2012.

Maxwell, Scott. "Nelson vs Mack: The Race That Never Really Got Going." *Orland Sentinel* November 6, 2012.

McDonald, Michael.United States Election Project. Calculations made from data in the United States Election Project.http://www.electproject.org/home/voter-turnout/voter-turnout-data. Accessed June 4, 2015.

Morrissey, Ed. "Can Gingrich's Challenge in Florida Succeed?" hotair.com/archives/ 2012/02/ 02/ can-gingrichs-challenge-in-florida. February 2, 2012.

Norrander, Barbara. "The multi-layered impact of public opinion on capital punishment implementation in the American states." *Political Research Quarterly* 53, no. 4 (2000): 771–793.

Open Secrets. 2012. "Florida Senate Race: 2012 Cycle." http://www.opensecrets.org/races/ indexp.php?id=FLS1&cycle=2012. Accessed June 4, 2015.

Pinsky, Mark. "Best Laid Plans." *Orlando Magazine*. http://www.orlandomagazine.com/Orlando-Magazine/February-2013/Best-Laid-Plans/February, 2013.

"President Exit Polls" *New York Times*. n.d. http://elections.nytimes.com/2012/results/president/exit-polls

Smith, Adam. "In Fierce Florida Senate Fight, It's Connie Mack vs Bill Nelson." *Tampa Bay Times*. August 14, 2012.

Sullivan, Sean. "Bill Nelson's Survival Strategy." *National Journal*. January 11, 2012.

Torres. "Florida State Senate District 12 Race 2012 – Frank's Notes." politics.com/2013/09/02/ florida-state-senate-district-12-race-2014-franks-notes/. September 2, 2013.

Index